MARY ROBERTS

14 Dogs & Me

One Woman's Story of Never Saying No

Dedication

There are over 3,500 animal shelters in the US as of 2022. There are also more than 14,000 rescue groups. Nearly a million shelter animals are euthanized every year. In 2011, it was nearly three million. This massive decrease in shelter deaths is due to the commitment of thousands of folks who work in shelters and rescues.

Without these workers who have dedicated themselves to making the lives of shelter and rescue animals better, there would be much more suffering. Blood would run through our streets as stray and surrendered animals are euthanized and buried in landfills.

My book is dedicated to the shelter and rescue workers who have stemmed the tide of needless death and changed millions of lives. I couldn't have written this book without them.

Contents

Introduction

Frida sits on one of the small boulders dotting the landscape, a bloodied snake at her feet. She's taking a break after redecorating the backyard with my yoga pants, flip-flops, rolls of toilet paper, the contents of my bathroom waste basket, and heads of daffodils.

I had been gone fifteen minutes.

After spending six thousand dollars on my yard last spring, I imagined pleasant outdoor gatherings with friends, enjoying the flagstone patio, the apple-blossom tree, shrubs with vibrant pink flowers, and tall native grasses.

Getting mad is useless. This is her home now and I'm pleased she feels comfortable enough to use my clothes as décor. But I know better. I've surrendered the backyard to this little dog just like I surrendered my house and my life to the thirteen dogs that preceded her.

"Come, Frida," I call to her. She moseys over only when I say the word "treat" and shake the treat jar.

I adopted Frida four months ago from a Wyoming rescue. She's a Jack Russell Terrier and Chihuahua mix—white with fawn-colored highlights and a heart-shaped spot on her left side. At eighteen pounds, her flanks are muscular, her waist narrow. Her ears are outsized periscopes, scanning her world for food, love, and unseen enemies. Her eyes, almond-shaped and dark, are rimmed with ancient kohl. I stare at her until she turns away, but I can't help it.

She's a canine Cleopatra. Beautiful, mysterious, and a skilled murderer. Frida preys on small animals and reptiles. I tell myself she'll calm down and give up her killing sprees once she realizes food and shelter are no longer her responsibility. After all, she was a pregnant stray and had to kill for food. None of us are free from our past and its consequences.

* * *

That was two years ago. The backyard slaughter continues unabated. Frida pounces on yellow neon garter snakes and baby bunnies, shaking them until blood spurts in all directions. She runs the fence, chasing the squirrels taunting her until one day she kills one of them—snapping its neck like a poorly-made stuffed toy.

Once we were walking along the Poudre River Trail and she leapt into the long grass bordering the trail, emerging with a screaming mouse in her jaws. I could hear its panicked squeaks.

"Eek! Eek!"

"Goddamn it, let go, Frida!" I shrieked, trying to pry the poor thing out of her mouth. I stepped on her feet. She yelped, the mouse tumbling to the ground. It was dead, its eyes and mouth still open. I'd been talking to my son Dan, a 4th year medical resident, and had dropped my cell phone in horror. He was still on the line.

"Mom, she's a terrier. That's her job," he said to me after I retrieved my phone.

Her job? Her job is to love me and listen to me occasionally.

Dan asked if the mouse was still breathing and maybe I should attempt resuscitation.

"I'll walk you through it," he says, "now that I'm a doctor."

I'm happy to give my son a good laugh but I hang up. At least my dogs don't make fun of me.

Frida is my fourth terrier mix. Two others were killers like her but not as efficient and satisfied with their work. I should've chosen a goofy Golden Retriever or a lazy yellow lab.

I never choose the dog, though. We find each other—in a chilly warehouse filled with dogs in crates needing adoption. Or standing on my porch, hoping there's room at the inn. And sometimes an aging and handsome yellow face stares out from my computer screen on Petfinder.com, his tongue inching up his nose.

That's how we found Dylan.

Dylan made me happy. He was lovely and kind and silly; I'd drop to the floor and hug his eighty pounds hard. Dylan was my ninth dog, but it was only when I was lying on the family room rug, listening to this big boy's heartbeat that I realized dogs had kept my heart from solidifying into the unforgiving mass it had every intention of becoming. Dogs were my statin, my anticoagulant, my pacemaker, allowing me to feel and give love.

Some say I have a chip on my shoulder; that I'm defensive, suspicious of a 'kind' word. It was my childhood, I say, distant, not safe from ridicule, bereft of affection, riddled with a stutter. But none of us kids escaped the residue of the ordinary damage incurred in a dysfunctional Irish Catholic household, trying to hold it together through the 1950's and '60's.

My ordinary damage was a fearful heart, refusing to read love stories or watch Christmas movies. Unless there was a dog involved.

The Buddhist teacher Dzigar Kongtrul Rinpoche wrote in his book, *Training in Tenderness*, "It's not hard to identify the tender heart in your own experience. For example, if you have a pet, you often feel strong affection in their presence ... seeing how your dog responds to your affection, how it wags its tail when you enter the room, gives you pure delight."

My dogs *do* delight me—despite their foibles and idiosyncrasies and ill manners. Despite the destroyed furniture and rugs, cars smelling like kennels, ruined vacuums, repairs to my fence, the nights at the doggie ER. Despite the thousands of dollars spent on toys, car seats, leashes, coats, supplements, training, physical therapy, doggie daycare. Despite the last ten years of New Year's Eves and 4th's of July spent at home, attempting to explain why humans need fireworks despite their effect on animals. Instead, they get thunder coats, hugs, and bison kneecaps.

Carolyn Knapp, who authored *Pack of Two*, says dogs offer "a kind of corrective emotional experience," helping to re-write the childhood script, though she worries she is becoming the "reclusive, dog-obsessed misfit, too fearful and damaged to live a 'real' life."

Like Knapp, I feared my dysfunctional childhood may have doomed me to the inevitability of being labeled 'The Crazy Dog Lady.'

But I need dogs. When I reach down to pick up a napping Chihuahua (carefully) or lie down to cuddle an old stinky lab on a ginormous dog bed—I feel better. When they open their eyes and sigh, then go back to sleep—I feel loved.

I'm not alone. There's a tribe of us who find the company of our dogs more easing than a human hug, more trustworthy and restorative than any medication. We decorate our homes with expensive dog beds, framed selfies with our dogs, and sculptures of dogs doing yoga. We celebrate holidays with gifts, special treats, and funny hats for our Buddys and Bellas, our Luckys and Lulus.

When we lose a dog to death or feel the need for *just one*

more, we walk the shelters or search online until we find a goofy black Lab or a terrified Rat Terrier waiting for us. Frida was neither goofy or terrified, but I knew she was destined to sleep in my bed and share my walks on the Poudre Trail minutes after we met. Kismet? Dumb luck? Karma? Like most choices in my life, I'm unable to explain it.

This is the story of me and the fourteen dogs that shared my life. They brought me joy and acceptance. I hope I did the same for them.

CHAPTER 1

ANGEL

1964

The smell wound its way up the stairs, slowly waking me. I thought it was me, unable to rouse myself enough to make it to the bathroom. It was Angel, our new puppy, downstairs crying and pooping uncontrollably. We used newspapers for the worst of it and wiped down the mudroom floor with bleach and old towels.

Angel had only been with us a few days when the vomiting and diarrhea started. Sometimes I remember her as a yellow lab mix, other times I remember a fluffy dog, like a Pomeranian or a Shih Tzu. Though I never considered us a fluffy dog kind of family.

I ran home from sixth grade all week to see if she was better until one day she was gone. Dad said she needed to see the doctor at the hospital. I waited a few days for her to come home. She didn't.

Angel was from the MSPCA[1]-Angell Memorial Animal Hospital in Boston, the oldest animal shelter in the country. It opened an intensive care clinic in the 1950's.

I imagined a handsome young veterinarian or maybe a grizzled older guy yelling out orders to vet techs valiantly trying to save Angel. Truth is, she probably died on the way there. She was barely moving when Dad lifted her carefully in a couple of towels and placed her in the passenger seat of our station wagon. He may have been the one to tell me they had a new surgical unit with vets hovering around the operating table. Or maybe he thought I'd forget about her.

Angel was our first dog. Her death convinced me our family had failed a test of our ability to care for young animals. How hard could it be? I know better, now, of course. She probably had giardia or parvo, maybe even distemper.

I didn't know how to feel. Another week with Angel and I would've handed over the keys to my emotional health to her. She would have the power to make me happy or destroy any sliver of self-esteem I might've had by choosing another kid for her best bud. That job would be handed over to other dogs.

Any memory of being comforted doesn't exist, but it could've happened. I'm sure Mom reached over and hugged me with one arm while she held a cigarette away from me with her other arm. I hope I leaned into her and accepted the embrace, but I can't be certain.

Other families had dogs that didn't die the first week they had it. Why didn't we take Angel to the doctor sooner? Other families had funerals for their animals and were sad for a while. How come we didn't do something like that? Maybe we fed her the wrong food or let her get into poison. Maybe we were just a terrible family. I was an unhappy child; I figured everyone else was unhappy, too. Maybe unhappiness was contagious, and it made Angel sick.

It wasn't time to ask for another dog and I didn't even know if I wanted one. But if I did, my expectations of how it would be were tempered. Like any lonely, depressed kid, I wanted someone to love who would love me back. It was simple as that. Dogs seemed suited to the task.

I watched my brothers, Billy and David, become close friends. Late at night they'd see who could fart the loudest without shitting the bed and I laughed into my pillow in my bedroom right next to theirs. I wanted that camaraderie with my older sister Kathleen, but that ship had long ago set sail and had gotten all the way to Perth, Australia—the farthest place on earth from Boston. The two youngest, Nancy and Nicky, were locked in an ancient battle for the last few scraps of attention from my parents. Depending how one counts, I shared second place with my twin Billy, or I was third, Billy having been taken from the womb a minute before me during the C-section. In patriarchal 1950's, I would never be equal to the first-born male. I would have to navigate this family solo.

I don't know why our family struggled with intimacy and trust, but like all Irish Catholic memoirists, I harbor half-assed theories and snippets of hurts and resentments.

When I began writing about my childhood, I sent away for any notes I could get from my year in therapy with a 'Dr. Camus,' a psychiatrist at Boston Children's Hospital. I put Camus in quotes because I'm not certain that was his name. I may have been reading Camus' *The Stranger* at the time. As if my stuttering didn't alienate me enough from the world, the book led me further down that hole. There were no notes from a 'Dr. Camus' or any psychiatrist, but there was a two-page report, filled with the scrawling of a social worker who had interviewed my mother and me and concluded a home visit would be appropriate. It never happened. I assume it was because Mom was a social worker, too, and had assured her interviewer that, despite what either of us had said—WE WERE FINE! But a specific quote from the long-ago report confirmed I wasn't harboring hallucinogenic memories of a questionable childhood.

"In general, Mrs. Roberts seems to have accepted (chaos) … as normal for a family of eight, though she did say she "wished some morning someone would come into the kitchen and say hello, drop dead, or something."

Mom wasn't going to allow anyone to come in and make judgments about her parenting skills.

I get it. Mom knew having an outsider come in to analyze our family, asking questions about our relationships and how we felt about each other, wasn't going to end well. In retrospect, it might have helped some of us, but I understand Mom's reluctance to 'air our dirty laundry.' You just didn't do that back then.

Maybe she hoped dogs would serve as an outlet for our affection, our need for acceptance and attention or love or whatever. There is one thing we all agreed on—dogs were going to be our salvation.

---

1. Massachusetts Society for the Prevention of Cruelty to Animals

CHAPTER 2
CASEY

1964

C asey arrived a few months after Angel's demise. He was another MSPCA-Angell Memorial rescue, a brown teddy bear with floppy ears and white patches. He was The Perfect Mutt, a blend of so many breeds, to guess his lineage would be futile.

He rollicked through the house, bouncing from kid to kid, room to room. The boys laid claim to him early. I didn't fight them—it was useless. Casey didn't stop running until collapsing on someone's bed dirty, wet, and exhausted. Obedience lessons would have been useful, but we just rode with him, chased him down the street, tackling him when he started to slow.

Occasionally, I got Casey to sleep in my bed, after begging my parents to tell my brothers Casey wasn't just *their* dog. Casey would snore fitfully beside me, his paws tremoring, dreaming of flights across meadows, chasing flickers and bugs, jumping in a river or shallow puddle. I'd watch him until we both grew silent, my arm around his body, his head on my pillow.

Casey ignored our family's fights and tears and shoving, wagging his tail maybe hoping to intervene when the shouting got too loud. Did he think living with us was better than the shelter he came from or the streets where they found him? We didn't have him long, so maybe it didn't matter.

Nothing could be done the night it happened. My twin brother Billy had ridden off on his bike to deliver the evening paper on a rainy New England dusk. At the last minute, he considered leaving Casey home, but that silly dog shot out the door when Billy picked up his canvas bag of newspapers, and it was decided. I grant Billy absolution and believe he just made a bad decision as a kid. I remembered some of what happened, but I never got the whole story. Until I recently called my brother and asked him, more than fifty years later.

He was crossing Great Plain Avenue and thought Casey was next to him. Great Plain was our main thoroughfare, but in a town of thirty thousand residents, we didn't consider it 'busy.' He looked back and saw Casey across the street. He called him. Casey ran in front of a car. It didn't stop. Billy heard the double thunk of its tires as it rolled over the dog. He remembers Casey trying to get up and drag himself over to where Billy stood screaming. Casey collapsed and lay in the road in the path of Needham residents trying to get home at 5:00 PM on a rainy night. I hope Casey never saw it coming or felt anything but a millisecond of pain. I hope he was running through the rain,

enjoying the wetness and the puddles and the absolute under-
standing this is what he was supposed to be doing.

A car pulled over and Mrs. Roman, who worked at the cafe-
teria in our school, ran out and stopped traffic. She managed to
place a call in the pre-cell phone era to her husband, a local
cop, who came right away and helped put Casey's body in the
trunk of her car. She hugged Billy and told him she would take
care of it. I never knew. It wasn't something I forgot; I just never
knew. Billy lives alone in a Buddhist mountain community now,
attending to the needs of a twelve-year-old dog and two semi-
feral cats, reluctant to leave behind their wildness but growing
more comfortable with sleeping in Billy's bed.

When I called to ask him about 'that day,' I hear him settle
in as he re-visits a painful afternoon. He told me he didn't go
home right away because he felt obligated to finish his paper
route, not wanting to get into trouble.

I remember him sobbing "he's dead, he's dead" when he
biked up our driveway. It could only have been Casey, for who
else would we lose ourselves to? Billy needed someone to hold
him and tell him he didn't do anything wrong, that it wasn't his
fault. I wanted to know where Casey's body was. Was he dead
or just headed to the vet? I didn't believe Billy, thinking he
knew nothing of death so how could he make such a declaration? My brother stood there, shivering. I went inside and
stayed in my room with my stuffed animals.

I don't know what happened when Billy told Mom and
Dad. Maybe Billy got a hug or a comforting arm around his
shoulders. I hope he didn't get yelled at or experience the wrath
of the other kids. Billy tells me he didn't want to do his homework that night, wanting to grieve or at least talk about what
happened. He had thought about asking to stay home the next
day from school, but he didn't. I don't remember talking about
it ever again. Just moments of grief for Casey, for my brother,

and my parents who had no idea how to handle their kids in the wake of the loss of a beloved dog.

For the rest of my life, when one of my dogs was near death and in pain, I'd wonder if they were afraid in their last few moments of life. I wanted to do something to alleviate their fear. Did they think I had abandoned them? Did they think I allowed this pain? As if I had a choice or the power to stop the hurt. Had anyone held Casey's head as he died, or had they stood apart, staring at him, wishing only to go back a few minutes in time and stop the unstoppable?

We grieved alone in our rooms, unable to grieve together. It was too much, we were too vulnerable.

I thought the word vulnerability meant being unarmed or having a flank exposed, a bad thing when one is in the middle of a war. I just never understood what war we were fighting. Did anyone blame Billy? I hope not.

We'll never know how long Casey would have lasted with us if he wasn't killed in the accident. Maybe he was just too wild, or we were too ignorant and careless. Once when driving, I hit a squirrel running in the middle of the road. I was sixty-five years old and had made it this long without knowingly killing an animal with my vehicle. I called Larimer Humane. They told me to leave it alone and let it die. They'd try and get someone by to pick it up. I cancelled my appointment and went home and lay in bed with my dogs.

I hope the person who hit Casey and took off is still tormented at night by the thump of a beautiful dog and the grief of a young boy.

I feel I should end this chapter with a kinder thought. But I can't think of one.

CHAPTER 3
TAFFY

1965-1977

It couldn't have been long after Casey died when we got Taffy. I hope it was long enough for us to weigh the consequences of getting another dog after having killed two others. Not on purpose, of course, but there was a carelessness about us, a lack of attention the Universe found distasteful. Its only recourse was to kill our dogs.

I was convinced there was a rumor racing around the animal rescue community, warning desperate puppies in shelters to take their chances on staying put rather than going home with the Roberts. As eager as I was to get another dog, it probably wasn't a good idea. For the dog.

If we were ever to get another one, my Dad would have to go incognito, or we'd have to send an emissary. Dad stopped for a moment and listened when I told him no one would give us a dog because of what happened to Angel and Casey. I had seen photos of Dad as a kid and his siblings with several dogs, all looking like the pit bulls we disparage today. More like the dog in "The Little Rascals." He doesn't remember where his family dogs came from, "Maybe someone's dogs had pups, who knows? Father always liked a dog or two." I never met my grandfather but I think I would've liked him. He said he didn't think all the dogs at the shelter were warning the staff to not let us in the door.

It was stupid, but dogs were magical to me. I needed a dog —to love, to love me back, to find comfort with, to be my best friend. A cat wouldn't do. I imagined a cat would walk away when it got bored or became uncomfortable with my neediness.

* * *

At fourteen years old, I knew if I didn't conquer my stutter my life would become a series of failures. I'd become a homeless bag lady pushing a grocery cart with blankets, bags of Twinkies and a carton of Marlboros. I was planning on taking up smoking as soon as I could get away with it. Both my parents smoked. It seemed a reasonable decision.

The bag lady scenario haunted me for years. When the housing market crashed in 2008, I was a real estate agent. The dream reappeared, only this time, there were three small dogs in the grocery cart and a huge bag of dog food on the shelf underneath. I can still picture the disapproving looks of those dogs, miffed at the loss of their multiple dog beds and large jugs of treats. I would lay in bed, imagining our walk of shame as we headed to the Mission, just yards from the happy sounds of people I knew listening to music in Fort Collins' Old Town Square.

Mom told us about her welfare clients with their kids or cats, hauling all their worldly goods in wagons or grocery carts. She said it would be our fate if we didn't come up with a plan or two to succeed in the world.

What's the plan when you believe you are incapable of speech? Back in the 1950's, educators conflated speech difficulties and mental or developmental disorders. I thought I was an idiot. What was the plan when you were essentially mute and had the IQ of a living room couch?

All six of us kids went to St. Josephs' Parochial School, where learning and discipline was equally dispersed by the Sisters of Charity of Halifax. After 8th grade, the boys headed to a Jesuit High School. Kathleen and I attended Elizabeth Seton High School. It didn't work out for either of us. I followed her to Needham High School where she was VP of her high school class and never skipped a day of school. The boys loved their high school. They played basketball and competed in their studies for the best grades. After graduation, Billy got a scholarship to Fordham to study journalism. David jumped into premed.

I, on the other hand, couldn't decide who I would marry— Micky Dolenz of The Monkeys or Little Joe of Bonanza fame. I figured they'd want me, too, once I achieved my dream of becoming a Rock Star or Broadway actress, or both. But there was no real plan, and I did nothing to make it happen.

I was just waiting for the next dog.

When Dad came home with Taffy, I assumed he went to another shelter, not wanting to be denied a dog by the staff at MSPCA-Angell Memorial. She was an Irish Setter/Golden Retriever mix who suffered our claustrophobic embraces, rolling her eyes and sighing in resignation, as we lined up to wait our turn for the privilege of crawling under the kitchen table where she hid. I worried someone would mistakenly crack one of her ribs or accidentally suffocate her.

"Mom, Mom, David is killing Taffy!" I'd yell upstairs after dinner when all Mom wanted was a smoke and a bath. I can still *feel* her eyes rolling.

"Mom, David's hugging her too tight! I think Taffy's dead!" Sometimes I'd just kick David or Billy under the table and run off.

Taffy was beautiful, regal, a bit dismissive. Or bored. I couldn't tell. She wasn't quite the goofy Golden Retriever or snooty Irish Setter. Broad of chest with shorter legs than the lanky setters, she had a deep red color with a blond undercoat impossible to recreate at a salon. Her hair defeated the dead-weight Hoover vacuums Mom loved.

Sixty-five years later, I want to apologize to Taffy for the various infractions our family incurred as dog owners. We never walked her—she walked herself, moseying over to friendly neighbors for treats and eventually downtown to the bakery. I don't remember having a leash or picking up dog poop. I do remember the mounds of dog poop everywhere in our small town. At least we weren't the only assholes.

We never took Taffy anywhere. We just let her in and out of the house. How did she not wander off into another neighborhood or town or just decide we were a crazy-ass family that needed psychiatric help and she wasn't going to be the in-house therapist? But she didn't leave us. She'd be gone for a bit then be home in time for dinner. Like us, I guess. We didn't leave either.

We also crammed eight people in the station wagon with no seat belts, carried babies in our laps in the front seat, and waved our parent's cigarette smoke away during dinner. Having your dog escorted home in a police car when she wouldn't leave her post at the front door of the local bakery wasn't a big deal then and maybe it shouldn't be now. My hometown isn't much bigger today. I hope the police still excuse the flagrant canine scofflaws who navigate traffic lights and sit in the Town Square begging for lunch. I hope some of those dogs get to ride in the back seat of a police car every so often.

When there are eight humans in a household, six of them irresponsible children, everyone assumes someone else fed and watered the dog. I feel a twinge of guilt because I don't remember doing much of that, but I do trust my mother. She always had a decent meal for us; there's no reason to believe she didn't do the same for the dog.

The worst thing we did to Taffy was to give her that name. We fought fiercely about it, until Mom picked the stupidest name and declared it done. I secretly tried other names on her when we were alone, but she was Taffy, identifying Mom as the pack leader and accepting her silly name. I wanted Rebecca or Maxine, more dignified as I imagined she would become.

As much as we all wanted to be Taffy's favorite, competitively calling her from different parts of the house to see who she'd come to, I don't think any one of my siblings could be declared 'the most loved.' Remembering our screaming contests, I feel even more shame we might have screwed her up as three or four voices shouted at her to "Come, Taffy, come!" I imagine she went outside and pretended she was deaf.

Taffy was the first in a long line of dogs that had my back but not in the usual sense, like Lassie. She wouldn't rescue me from bullies or pull me from the path of a speeding car or even choose me as her bedmate when night fell. She'd go with anyone, and we'd often have fights over that, too.

"You had her last night!"

"Well, she hates you!"

"You're an idiot!"

"*Taffy* thinks you're an idiot!"

"Your farts are going to kill Taffy!"

We'd try to steal Taffy from a sibling's bed if they had fallen asleep. Some nights she'd end up sleeping in three or four different beds until declaring enough was enough and she wasn't moving again. We did the same thing with the one radio in the house. The best of all was to sneak into someone's room who was already asleep and steal the double prize—the radio and the dog.

She had my back in the best way possible. When I was with Taffy, I could speak. Close to fluent as I'd ever been. I told her the stories I wanted to tell my family or a friend. She wouldn't make fun of me, even if the story was just about Katie Fitzgerald teasing me on the basketball court the nuns had set up in the parking lot.

"P-p-p-pass me the b-b-ball, M-m-m-mary," she'd yell at me while holding up her hands with the audacity to think I would throw her the ball after she made fun of my stutter. Hurling the ball at her fat face would give me satisfaction, but Sister Ann Patricia had other ideas as she ordered me to pass the ball to her. I had to. Sister Ann had a clear shot.

I'd get up and show Taffy how Sister Ann made the basket, her right hand slowly releasing the ball, her wrist bent, lingering over her head as if it were guiding the ball into the net. Swish! No net! It was worth it not throwing the ball at Katie, I'd tell Taffy, and if I had hurled the ball at Katie, I probably would've missed.

Taffy and I read together in the long summer New England afternoons. She'd lay next to me on the wide window seat of my bedroom, her dark red head resting in my lap, as I read aloud from Poe's *The Cask of the Amontillado*.

Fortunato had hurt me a thousand times and I had suffered quietly.

But then I learned that he had laughed at my proud name ...

I promised myself that I would make him pay for this—that I would have

revenge.

Not once did I stumble, clench my jaw, or feel like throwing up. I was fluent, even poetic, my voice rising and falling with the words as Poe intended. After an anxious day spent hiding from the world, hoping to not be noticed, coming home to Taffy and a book was my sanctuary.

I believed we needed each other to survive in our household. For her, it was a respite from the bickering, for me it was a chance to speak slowly, without feeling I'm taking up too much of someone's time. Anyone with a speech impediment knows the feeling. Hell, *I* had a hard time listening to me. It's not about self-pity or bemoaning the past or the burdens we carry. I've worked through most of it, and I only mention it now because Taffy saved me from going further down the rabbit hole I assumed would be my forever home. I may have avoided the deepest end of that rabbit hole, but as author and stutterer John Whittier Treat says—"My stutter has receded over time but the worst of it has made me who I am."

The Taffy photo I remember most is her sitting on our back-porch stairs. The ten steps are wide; a human family of thirty or more could fit on those stairs but when Taffy was on them, they were hers. In this photo, my dog from college, Demian, sits a few steps down and Taffy stares straight at the camera while Demian's face is caught either in a yawn or a growl. Taffy isn't impressed with her new companion, and I don't remember ever bringing Demian back to the homestead again.

Taffy had one canine friend, Gunnar, the three-legged Golden Retriever down the street. I fantasized about them running off to the bakery together to eat creampuffs and lemon tarts. Taffy preferred her lone walk to Needham Bakery and waited patiently outside until someone came out and gave her a sweet pastry or a lick of meringue. Gunnar visited us on occasion but respected Taffy's domain and her people, though one of my brothers, David, became enamored of the handsome retriever and it may have affected his relationship with Taffy. He was looking toward the future and which colleges he should choose, so maybe he didn't have time anymore to nap under the kitchen table with Taffy and assure her of his allegiance.

How do dogs survive dysfunctional households? Taffy's favorite place was under the table while our lives swirled around her. Her next place was the couch in the living room, which still afforded her a view of the coming and goings in the kitchen but at a less dangerous outpost.

A week before I was to start driving lessons in high school, I was in a car accident, putting me in the hospital for a month. I was not the driver. It was the beginning of summer vacation in 1968, just before my senior year.

Taffy and I spent two months moving from couch to bathroom and back to couch and then, with a little help from a friend, out to the yard where I lay prone and sweaty on a chaise lounge with those plastic, sticky vinyl straps until my friend got back from summer school classes. Taffy lay in the shrubs then moved to the porch when the summer sun hit the noon mark, but she never abandoned me. We became compatriots, a country of two, sworn to keep a wary eye on the rest of the world, protecting our fellow citizen.

My siblings weren't around for most of that summer. The boys caddied at Wellesley Country Club and rode bikes and then played basketball the rest of the day. Kathleen had left for Cape Cod in late May to spend the summer waitressing. Nancy and Nicky were around, but they are vague shadows appearing and disappearing just outside my three-feet-in-any-direction universe.

One afternoon, when my friend Joan had returned to bring me back inside, the sweat trickling down both my elbow and leg casts, Nicky and Nancy began an episode of their daily war.

This time Nick brought the hose inside the house to retaliate for some shitty remark made by Nancy and her friend. Nick chased them up the stairs and as far up the attic as the hose would go, soaking the wallpaper and the carpet. I would say I can't imagine his rage at so young an age, but I can.

I had crutches and hobbled after them while Taffy followed, until the water started flying. She retreated outside, preferring the heat of the day to an accidental spray of cold water. At 6'1", Joan took the stairs two at a time and wrestled the hose from Nick. He put up a good fight despite his age. Anger is a mighty muscle. She nearly lost.

Mom came home to a staircase of dangling wallpaper, its glued-on grip lost to a torrent of water. We did our best to mop up the stairs and rugs in the hallway. But it was a godawful mess. I imagine she thought we were feral children, unable to handle the responsibilities of being human.

Staying in defensive mode was the only way to survive in our household. Kind words were suspicious. And yet, there were moments when we were a team, laughing together, finding a bond in humor and the antics of a dog. In flashes of these moments, we realized we were family. We didn't identify as siblings as a rule, as people who would be there when the world turned on you. When I tell people about our childhood, they don't understand. "But you're all so close in age!" comes their observation as if blood and a couple of years apart were the only qualifications necessary to become the Cleaver family of *Leave it to Beaver* fame.

The two oldest boys were close, sharing a room and both attending a small Jesuit high school. I envied them. I didn't have an ally in the household and sought out Taffy whenever I saw my chance to be alone with her.

* * *

There are two things in my life whose threads have wound themselves so profoundly and intricately into my being that I've never seen a vision of a future without them.

They are dogs and Bruce.

We met in art class when I was a sophomore, and he was a senior. Already an accomplished sculptor, Bruce laughed at my attempts to create anything resembling 'art.' I took art only because it was one of the few classes that didn't require speaking. Most afternoons, we'd meet on the concrete steps in front of the high school, light up cigarettes and walk over to Bergson's, the local soda shop, ordering coffee milkshakes and French fries. I could talk to Bruce, not as freely and eloquently as I did with dogs, but it wasn't as painful as it was with other people, even my family. It was enough for me. It got easier as the year passed.

He was supposed to graduate and leave me, but who were 'we' anyway? Arm-punching buddies, smoking Marlboros by the football bleachers, making fun of players and the cheerleaders. I knew I didn't have a chance, but we had 'this.' Like everything else with him, it had to be enough.

I don't remember knowing Bruce didn't graduate because he refused to write his senior thesis. If he had asked, I would have written it for him. He spent another year at Needham High School, and he didn't seem one bit unhappy about it. Neither was I.

He did finally graduate the day before my accident.

While I was in the hospital, Bruce stopped by my room so many times his girlfriend came by to see what the hell was the big deal. I watched her walk into my room with a card or maybe flowers or maybe nothing. Susie was her name.

"Hi Mary, just wanted to see how you were," she smiled sweetly with her perfect dark hair, her straight teeth, her A-line skirt, white summer blouse and a pale pink cardigan, its arms wrapped around her shoulders, at the ready if she stayed long enough for the air conditioning to chill her precious body. I don't recall speaking more than three words to her *ever*. Popular member of the best high school sorority, a cheerleader, we did not mingle in the same crowd. Not that I mingled. I usually just slunk. I wore white-cotton collared shirts with rolled-up sleeves, too-long bell bottom jeans and sneakers. I was James Dean with braces and the not-cool, black-framed glasses.

"Hi Susie." I think I asked what she was doing there but don't remember what she said. She may have mentioned Bruce told her I was in the hospital. I don't know if she knew he spent every afternoon he could with me, careening around the hospital halls in my wheelchair, smoking cigarettes, and drinking the coffee milkshakes he brought with him. Susie and I had nothing to say to each other and she left after a few minutes.

My heart pounded and I tried to breathe normally. Did this mean she thought me worthy of jealousy? Did I threaten her? Did Bruce 'like' me? More than a friend 'like,' but someone who he might date for real, not just hanging out on the back porch with Taffy or filling up my hospital room with smoke or riding out to Rosemary Lake listening to "Brown-Eyed Girl."

I imagined Susie shaking her head in disbelief as she walked away thinking she may have to worry about me stealing her boyfriend. All I could think of was Bruce kissing me for the first time. It would be awkward—we would smile, then fall into a tender embrace where he would express his love and say he was just waiting for me to mature past a sixteen-year-old Catholic girl's fear of anything intimate or gross.

When I told Bruce Susie had been by, he laughed. Out loud. So, I did too.

After my hospital stay, he still came by the house a couple of times a month, but by then he was a student at The Boston Museum School of Fine Art and had an apartment and a new artist girlfriend. Yet he never missed a holiday with us, sitting around the kitchen table talking to Mom, who'd flick her cigarette in an ashtray and tell him to cut his hair.

The day before I left for college in New York he was there, pulling up in the driveway in his Jeep to say goodbye and tell me he would see me at Thanksgiving. Our trips across town, listening to music, and smoking Marlboros continued when I was home for vacation and his girlfriend was visiting her family. We never discussed her.

Southampton College in Long Island, New York was not for me. In the fall of 1970, after my freshman year, I moved back home to Needham and sat on the side porch of my childhood home smoking cigarettes and hugging Taffy. Bruce was at my house within a couple of days, grinning in the driveway, jumping out of his Jeep, and bounding through the screen door. I don't know how he found out I was home. But from then on, I'd look out my window every night, waiting for him to show up while he went on with his life and mine was at a standstill.

A friend of Mom's got me a job in Medical Records at Boston Children's Hospital. Its vast stores of patient records were in the basement where I'd wander all day, plucking out files and delivering them to the different floors of the hospital. The worse one was the pediatric burn ward.

I hated this job. I also hated riding the subway every day, competing for a seat or a bit of space for my hand on a steel pole that would save me from being flung across someone's lap.

When a guy slipped his hand down my pants while I stood crushed between fellow subway riders, both arms clutching a ceiling strap, I froze, afraid to bring attention to myself. Would people laugh? Would they think I was making a big deal out of nothing? It seems unbelievable now, but I did nothing.

As soon as I got off at my stop and started climbing the big hill to the hospital, I decided to move to Colorado. Humiliated and angry, I strode into work and stood outside my manager's office trying to decide what to say. She invited me in, and I sat uncomfortably, finally blurting out I was quitting because I was moving to Colorado. My sister lived there and people in Boston were terrible, and I was a chicken shit. It's what I wanted to say but I only told her my sister Kathleen lived in Fort Collins, Colorado with a bunch of girls and dogs and there was a room open for me if I wanted it.

Truth was, I was leaving Massachusetts because Bruce was there. Bruce of high school, Bruce of the long blonde hair and blue eyes, Bruce of Marlboro Country, of art class, of late nights spent driving around our hometown, smoking cigarettes, and listening to music in his Jeep CJ-5. Bruce of friend territory, of sitting on our back porch talking late into the night after he dropped off his girlfriend.

I had to leave. My sister Kathleen had transferred to Colorado State University in Fort Collins, Colorado after spending a lonely summer in her room with mono. Mom was still mad at her for getting caught shoplifting with old high school friends a couple of weeks after she got home from her first year at Mt. St. Vincent, a Catholic college for women in upstate New York. It was the first time Kathleen had ever done anything remotely wrong. She even received a certificate for never missing one day of school from kindergarten through high school.

Mom's expectations for Kathleen were huge and burdensome. Would a shoplifting charge keep her from law school? Would she end up a hardened criminal in prison smoking cigarettes and drinking toilet wine? Pretty sure that's where Mom's mind went.

According to a recent interview with my sister, "none of my siblings came to see how I was." I know how she feels but we were a dysfunctional family and visiting the ill, especially family, wasn't in our repertoire. And maybe we didn't want to get sick ourselves.

She decided there's no reason to stay near her family. Kathleen had one of those massive college catalogues and opened to a place called Fort Collins. Two months later, she flew to Denver and started her sophomore year at Colorado State University.

It was 1969. Woodstock, LSD, Frank Zappa concerts in NYC, moon landing, draft lottery, Vietnam March on Washington, and all hell was breaking loose. I always thought Kathleen may have experienced a vision of the future, standing on the sidelines with her pale pink shirtwaist dress, sensible flats and a working knowledge of the Catholic doctrine and decided she had had enough of being the good girl. I didn't know she was hurt by her family's lack of compassion.

My sister arrived in Colorado in time for the Rolling Stones and BB King Concerts in November 1969 then the burning of Old Main, a revered building on campus, during the Kent State protests in May the following year.

She came home for Christmas in 1970 and said there was an extra room in her house in Fort Collins, and I could take it if I wanted.

The night before I left for Colorado, Bruce came over and we sat around the kitchen table with Mom and smoked and drank vodka tonics for a couple of hours until Mom went to bed. I walked Bruce out to his Jeep. It was so cold. He smelled like smoke and art supplies and clean hair. If this were a Nicholas Sparks novel, there would be a different ending. Bruce would pull me close and beg me to stay. I'd weep for joy then rush back inside and call the airlines, cancelling my flight the next morning.

He held my hand and asked if Colorado was what I wanted. I shrugged my shoulders.

"Of course, it isn't, you fool of a man!" I wanted to shout. But I didn't.

He got back in the car and told me to get in the house, "It's cold, Mary. You'll get sick before you even get to Colorado."

I couldn't move. I stayed in the driveway until he backed up and drove back to his artist life and his artist girlfriend and what I assumed was the perfect life filled with inspirational sculptures, visionary art friends, and pretty girls with their exquisite faces and bodies.

I've had much time to replay this moment in my head.

Years later, I admitted to him I felt I wasn't good enough for him, I didn't know anything about art or Boston. I was afraid to drive or walk downtown near his apartment at night. Any cool factor I possessed was eclipsed by my stutter, my fear of driving, my inadequacy around anything to do with creativity, my lack of an iota of self-esteem. I was afraid I would disappoint him, and our romance for the ages would fizzle in a few months. We would barely make it to the next Christmas. He said he was afraid, too, then. Afraid I would have disdain for his lack of writing skills or something almost as stupid as my fears. We were such cowards.

CHAPTER 4
DEMIAN

1971-1983

K athleen and I flew into Denver, CO on New Year's Eve
1970. We took a bus from the old Stapleton Airport
north sixty miles to a very a cold, snowy night in Fort Collins.
Or at least I thought it was cold. I once Googled the weather,
and it said it was unusually warm and temperate. My memory
is of a struggle through a blizzard to get to Kathleen's shared
house on South Sherwood Street where we were denied entry.
It was locked during the Christmas vacation and Kathleen had
no key. She went next door and called a friend for help, and he
managed to break into the house.

The potential mistaken memory makes me an unreliable narrator or maybe a keen interpreter of situations fraught with terror. The struggle from the bus station, slipping and sliding down the street with our enormous suitcases amidst a dark and cold snowy night, was a metaphor for the fear and apprehension I felt moving in with my sister.

My sister and I were not best friends. She's only eighteen months older than I am and we should have been closer. But I was one of two at birth and I can imagine how stressful it was to no longer be the apple of your parents' eye. Soon there would be three more siblings. We were all wary of each other; it couldn't be helped.

There were already four or five girls living at that house, three with dogs. I suspected Kathleen had told them shit about me because I never felt welcome. I needed a dog, preferably a Taffy clone.

It was an ad in the Collegian newspaper, 'FREE PUPPIES!' and then the words 'golden mix.' I called and from the description over the phone, I envisioned another Taffy, dark red and noble but more affectionate. When the people drove up to the house and dumped a black Springer Spaniel/Lab mix on the porch, I was shocked. I couldn't demand my money back. She was free. They jumped back in the car and drove off.

It wouldn't be the last dog that sauntered into my life without an invitation, or at least with an invitation but unaccompanied by full disclosures.

I named her Demian because I was reading Herman Hesse's book *Demian: The Education of Emil Sinclair* at the time. Demian was Emil's mentor and 'daemon' or spiritual advisor in a time of confusion and despair for the protagonist. Did I think Demian would lead me through the dark days of my twenties, helping me through bad relationships and even worse career decisions? A muse to Lost Souls, Sister Canine Goddess to Delusional Young Women with Low Self-Esteem?

It was a lot for one dog.

Until the movie—*The Omen*—came out in 1976 and Damien, the anti-Christ, entered our lexicon. When asked her name, I'd confess it, then inform the inquisitive lout I named her after the Herman Hesse novel, NOT the terrifying movie about evil. It didn't help that Demian shunned most people and all dogs, once showing her teeth to an especially curious Lhasa Apso puppy. The owner called my dog "deranged" for threatening to harm such a cute little thing. I'm ninety-nine percent confident she wouldn't have hurt the pup. But that damn movie did worm its way into my consciousness, questioning whether I was raising the canine equivalent of the Devil's offspring.

She wasn't a dog people cooed over. She wasn't cuddly or interested in sitting on the couch with my arms around her or even spooning on the bed though she insisted on sleeping on it, just not too close.

Demian was me, and on an unconscious level I must have known. I never had many friends and they rarely blossomed into 'best friend' status. I could have used a good therapist back then to deal with my trust issues and lack of confidence, but I blamed it on being a Bostonian and coming from a strange and enigmatic family. I was without the resources to understand there was a good chance I would spend my life alone.

Demian reminded me of Greta Garbo and her famous line, "I vant to be alone." I suppose it was me, too.

Her long Springer ears *did* give her a sultry movie star look. Coupled with a lustrous ebony coat with gorgeous feathers and what I thought were soulful eyes expressing wisdom and compassion, we strutted our stuff on campus, no one protesting when I took her to class and my work-study obligation at the journalism department. She snored and farted through my journalism law final. I was politely asked to do something about it. I left. I wasn't going to pass anyway.

Memory slips here, but if there were complaints about

Demian wandering the halls of the journalism department, I don't recall. The photography professor objected, and I had to leave her with someone else when I spent time in the dark room. Something about dog hair. Were there impatient sighs and "Oh, shits" whenever I walked into a classroom? I ignored them if there were. I couldn't imagine leaving Demian at home. A few years later, the university implemented a NO DOG policy in classrooms. I'm confident Demian and I had something to do with that.

In today's language of emotional instability, I would be diagnosed with anxiety and PTSD and Demian would be my emotional support dog. Like Taffy, she was my opening to fluent speech. My hand would find its way to the top of her skull whenever I felt the familiar tightening of my jaw, then they'd slide down her long silky ears and I'd roll the velvet feathers between my fingers. Demian would grunt in what I hoped was happiness and I'd relax.

Those ears, while lovely in their Sophia Lorensque waves, became Demian's Achilles' Heel. During the summer, some of us would hike down the dam along Horsetooth Reservoir with our dogs for a late afternoon swim, hoping we'd be the only beings to inhabit a small cove with a beach cozy enough for just us. Demian was an adequate swimmer but didn't take joy in it like the goofy labs of my friends. I'd fold up her ears and attach them together with a clothespin after her swim in a desperate attempt to avoid the inevitable infection which I finally addressed with an operation when she was seven and I had some money.

In the spring of 1972, Kathleen and I moved to a farmhouse on North Taft Hill Road with an old barn and a tall skinny guy named Tom who had the best bedroom. It was nearly three miles to campus. I had no driver's license and no car. But Kathleen did, and I was able to hitch rides with her occasionally. Most of the time, Demian and I hitchhiked or biked, warily watching the cows across the street who'd gather in a scrum, staring at us as we moved down the street. It feels foolish now to confess I was afraid of cows, but what did I know?

By now, Kathleen had decided she, too, needed a dog. The first one, Caliban, the 'freckled monster' from Shakespeare's *The Tempest*, had a series of warts populating his mouth. What did she think would happen naming him Caliban? He was a pitiful little thing who was killed by a car when he was young. But not before he impregnated our roommate's dog. And thus, begat 'Moonie Moon' or officially Moonshine. Kathleen took the pup as payment for sperm from a dead dog. I don't understand why people refuse to spay or neuter their dogs.

I asked Kathleen for more memories of Moonie Moon while writing this chapter. She told me about the time when she had gone home for a while and took Moonie only to have her birth thirteen pups underneath Mom's bed. I had no idea. Or I forgot. Both are possible.

Fortunately, Moonshine had become Demian's best friend and, God knows, she needed one. A canine friend, I mean. I was her best friend.

I don't talk much about the guys in my life and their relationship to Demian. She was always put off by their presence, but with time and treats allowed them to pet her. I let her find her way with guys—it was always going to be her decision whether she showed her affable side or the one where she didn't give a shit if you were there or not. She was never mean or unpredictable. The less-affable dogs came later in my life; it was a good thing since it was also when men pretty much fell off the face of the earth for me.

* * *

We were living in the Taft Hill house when Bruce came to find me.

It was April 1972 when Bruce hitchhiked to Fort Collins, arriving at eleven o'clock one night on the outskirts of town. A few guys in a pickup stopped for him. He told them he was looking for a girl but didn't know where she lived. They suggested he get high and drove to their favorite pot dealer. It was a house a few blocks down from ours. Kathleen was dating the dealer and opened the door, only to find Bruce, standing in the doorway. She drove him to our house. Sometimes that's just how things happen.

I was home studying for a Botany mid-term with my new friend, Deni.

Kathleen came through the door and announced I had a surprise visitor. Bruce stood there in the frame of the doorway, not quite inside, grinning and tired, shifting his backpack off his shoulder and stepping into the house to lay it on the kitchen floor. This was the dream I visited weekly—Bruce would profess his undying love for me and take me back to Boston where we would start our lives together as a couple.

But I had a boyfriend, Larry. He was moody and quiet, though funny and a decent writer. He was also a DJ for the college station and knew about the best music coming out LA and NY from his friends who had chosen lives in big cities. He was easy and didn't care if I couldn't drive or had a little stuttering problem. Or he never told me if he did.

But I wanted Bruce. I wanted my 'soulmate' to be him. I just didn't trust we would grow up and figure it out. That night Bruce told me he wanted to be with me and have me come home with him to Boston where we would be together. I wasn't ready. I had a boyfriend. I kept telling him I couldn't transfer college credits again. Besides, Boston University wouldn't accept me. I was looking for him to tell me he loved me, and we would make it work. But he was afraid, too.

The next morning, I went to Larry's apartment and told him Bruce was here and I wouldn't be back until Bruce was gone. It was spring break. We had plans which I had just obliterated. Larry got on his motorcycle and left.

I went back to my house and told Bruce we could be together for the week.

Our first kiss was more urgent than romantic. Five years—five fucking years!—we had been wanting this. I think I cried. I'm sure he did, too. He still smelled like paint and wood and the road. Demian jumped on the bed and refused to move.

I was alternately in bliss and in despair, not wanting it to end but knowing it would because neither of us had the courage to lay it on the line. I picture us both reaching into our chests, wrenching our hearts from their place behind the breastbone and in-between the lungs and placing them bloody and pumping on the table, risking it all to show how we felt. We had loved each other since I was fifteen and he was seventeen, but it remained a secret to us both for reasons that could only be explained if we took hallucinogenics in a therapy session and bared our souls. If only we had. We were both afraid of losing ourselves to the other and never finding our way back. I was never sure why we had to find our way back—to what?

Yet I knew if we tried and it didn't work out, I wouldn't have the resources to survive it.

Demian behaved like Lassie during the week Bruce was with us, tail wagging, attentive, responsive to my requests. She even jumped on the couch looking to cuddle. I told Bruce, "She's never like this! She's usually doesn't give a shit!" We'd laugh, and Bruce said he didn't believe me. He thought Demian was a great dog, "Like Taffy," he said. "Laid back even when everyone was acting crazy."

I don't even remember what we did that week. Except hitchhike to campus and walk downtown, make dinner at the house, and pretend we were together forever. And then he had to leave.

I'm still uncomfortable playing the memory of Bruce

walking away along Taft Hill on his way out of town, sticking his thumb out while the cows stared at him from across the street. He wanted me to come back to Boston as soon as I could, so we could start dating or what? I didn't know. He didn't say. But I was unsure, worried I wouldn't measure up … up to what? What was 'what?'

Demian growled at the cows, warning them to stay in their own yard. I was distracted for a moment. A pickup screeched to a halt. Bruce turned to me to say goodbye and jumped in the cab of the truck. The last thing I saw was Bruce sitting in the passenger seat, looking back, and waving at us. I held my hand up, perfectly still. It was snowing. I was a snow woman, frozen in place, unable to find the courage to run after my heart.

I walked back to the house with Demian. I put the piece of rope I used for her leash on her, gathered my backpack loaded with schoolbooks and headed back to where Bruce had just disappeared and put my thumb out for a ride. I had classes to get to. Spring break was over.

What have I done? I looked at Demian on the floor of the old pickup truck that had stopped to give us a ride. The driver wanted my dog in the back, but it was snowing. I said no and settled her on the floor at my feet where we would stare at each other for the ride to campus—traumatized, as if we had survived a tornado or an invasion or just made the worst decision of our lives. Technically, it was my decision, but she didn't say anything when I told Bruce to go.

Demian and I had a few adventures over the next few years, and when I look back, I can only ask for her continued absolution as she checks in on me periodically from her perch on the Rainbow Bridge. Maybe it was the combination of youth and ignorance, but I was a shit dog owner. I left her with one bag of dog food and her dog bowl at a friend's house when I went on World Campus Afloat for five months. I walked her when it suited me. There were days I was gone for too many hours and

I'd come home to her sleeping on the couch with a full bladder and a disappointed look on her face. What did I do with her when I went on weekend trips? Did I even get her vaccinations? I'm hoping it's my memory that's deficit and not me.

I'm certain my dog-at-large case was the first one brought to municipal court in Fort Collins. In the summer of 1973, we were told to start leashing our dogs or there would be fines. Not having the money to buy a decent leash, I pulled down the clothesline, wrapped half its twelve feet around my hand and elbow and biked to campus with Demian trotting alongside. It wasn't far, maybe a quarter of a mile, but I was always late and the run was good for Demian.

On the way back, a huge Great Dane dragging a rope attached to a substantial branch ripped from its moorings rushed us from my right side. I had spotted the dog running around, struggling to release what looked like a thirty-pound log dragging behind him. We were just a half a block away when I braked hard, reeling Demian in as fast as I could. Jumping off the bike, I tossed it down between the Great Dane and us while undoing the long clothesline attached to Demian, screaming at her to go home, a block away. Surprisingly, she did. Behind me was a cop sitting in the driver's seat of his car. I gestured that the Dane was about to eat me, and would he please open the fucking door?

He rolled the window down and said he couldn't let me in, but he had called Animal Control. The Great Dane was sniffing my bike or I would've grabbed it and rode home.

Two minutes later the guys from Larimer Humane show up armed with oversized dogcatcher nets. The dog was young and afraid, and it didn't take long to subdue him. Meanwhile, Demian had circled back and sat beside me watching the shenanigans. It was sweet, "She just wanted to make sure I was okay," I told the officer, touched Demian would do such a thing. He handed me a ticket for dog-at-large.

I got an attorney. He was a friend of a friend and said he would do it for free. We ended up dating for a couple of months, though I insisted on writing him a check for one hundred dollars. It was never cashed.

My friends sat in court on a hot August day wearing their Catholic school wool kilts and cotton T-shirts. They thought a skirt might be more respectful and my attorney had asked them to look decent. Pairing them with T-shirts may not have been the best idea, but it showed they were trying. The cop didn't remember my twelve-foot clothesline or that I had stopped to unleash Demian and send her home and was thrilled she came back to see if I had been eaten by the Great Dane. He said I lied.

I was terrified to get on the stand, convinced I'd humiliate myself and stutter through the entire testimony. Stuttering would help my case but at great cost to my pride. The judge was solicitous and mentioned he too had a female dog and hated it when male dogs chased them on their walks when she was in heat.

Every so often, I take a second or two after I hear an ignorant statement before I lecture someone on their witlessness—this was one of those times. I wanted to tell the judge my dog was certainly spayed like any responsible dog owner would do, and parading your in-heat dog around town was ludicrous and frankly, reckless. Instead, I nodded, knowing if I had called him out like I was calling out the cop, this wouldn't end well. Growing up in the 50's, 60's and 70's, women knew the male ego could take only so much.

"Yes, your honor, it's scary when a male dog isn't restrained and chases Demian." I said, stuttering a little to great effect though not on purpose. I stared at the cop from my place of honor on the witness stand. He stared right back. I won, of course, but on the way out, the cop came up to us and said he would get me eventually. Grabbing my attorney's arm, I told him the cop just threatened me. Nothing anyone could do. I was marked. So was my dog. We moved, again.

Demian and I went through a few boyfriends for the next ten years. Felix was the longest. He had the tiniest and most delicate Doberman named Kizzy after Kizzy Kinte in the series *Roots*. Demian put aside her contrariness when it came to Kizzy, and for six years she endured raft trips, started running with me which I suspect she hated, moved to San Francisco right near the corner of Haight Ashbury, rode the city buses with a required muzzle, and hiked its parks. Demian settled into being a great dog. She loved Felix and Kizzy, but she didn't take to anyone else, except Moonie Moon, my sister's dog.

The job market was tough in San Francisco in the late 1970's and neither Felix nor I could secure a good-enough job to justify staying there. We eventually moved back to Fort Collins and bought a house together. Felix was a welder and river guide. It wasn't the life I wanted. I don't think he did either. We should've gone to couples' therapy and worked out our insecurities about each other and the life we were careening toward— but instead I asked him to leave.

I couldn't tell him I feared being poor and unhappy my whole life. I wanted to travel and have a great car that didn't break down and not worry about paying the utilities. Felix had his own stuff about self-worth and job insecurities. We were a mess, and we couldn't figure it out. He must have hated me.

* * *

Dad left Mom when I was in college in Colorado. He had taken over my bedroom by then and that's where Taffy slept at night. During the day, they sat on the living room couch together, Dad's arm wrapped around Taffy's neck, reluctant to abandon her but knowing he was already out the door. I want to believe leaving her broke his heart. I know it broke hers.

A few years later, it came time for Mom to pack up and leave the huge New England Colonial on May Street that witnessed so much dysfunction. There were happy times, too, especially when we were older and understood not everyone in the world waited to toss a winged barb that found its target too easily. We came home for holidays and the occasional summer week, hoping to get to the Cape to swim in the Atlantic and lie on the simmering dunes, reading and checking our tans. One Christmas vacation we smoked weed and went to movies to a showing of *The Exorcist*. We were remarkably high. I held my sister down in her seat when she got too scared and tried to leave. It was mean but hilarious.

I got the call to come home from Colorado and help Mom unearth twenty-five years of debris left behind by six kids. Taffy could no longer navigate the long staircase to Mom's room. She stayed on the main floor, sleeping on the couch, missing the presence of her all too human family.

Mom was moving into a condo that didn't allow dogs and it had stairs. At fifteen years old, Taffy was no longer able to freely roam the streets or follow kids. Arthritis and loneliness may have hastened her decline but when she looked at me with an acceptance and maybe a request, I understood then the final trip to the vet became my responsibility. In inhabiting the false bravado I showed the world, I convinced Mom I was able to 'do the deed' without having a nervous breakdown.

Nancy and her boyfriend came by to pick up Taffy and me. None of us had done this before. We were quiet. I remember smoking a cigarette, sitting in the backseat, blowing the smoke out the car window, my other arm around Taffy.

We walked into the vet's office. A young gal took Taffy in the back. We paid up front. That was it. No last moments in a room alone with her or a sedative in case Taffy panicked. No me holding her head in my arms. No recounting memories of a dog's antics and what a marvel of a being she had been. No sympathies from a vet and the staff or offers on cremation, returning our beloved in a pretty box with her ashes and a paw print.

But back then, like the fathers who paced nervously in the waiting area for the arrival of their baby, separated from the nitty-gritty and heart-rendering experience of birth, we left Taffy alone with strangers to die. I still ask for her forgiveness. Ignorance is no excuse, I say. I should have known better.

When my youngest sibling, Nick, found out what happened while he was at college, he yelled at Mom and called me a murderer.

I believe dogs have no fear of death and they possess knowledge of the afterlife, giving them the confidence to ask their humans to let them go. Or not. I have no idea. Over the following decades, as I watched my dogs suffer through surgery, peritonitis, debilitating spinal degeneration, acute pancreatitis, cancer, and a stroke, I came to understand fear of death doesn't exist for them. Fear of thunderstorms, fireworks, the big stick lying across the bike trail, swimming, and Halloween masks scared the hell out of a few of my dogs, but dying meant a release from pain and possibly a transition to the next family. I wonder who Taffy got. I hope they give her pastries every so often.

* * *

I flew back to Colorado and a new job and eventually a new relationship. I started dating my boss, Jay. Within a couple of years, I married him and Demian was a reluctant flower girl for our wedding in the back yard of our house in Old Town, the oldest part of the city. Demian laid down and snored during the short ceremony. I had run her in the morning a couple of hours before the wedding along Mountain Avenue, through a cemetery and back again. Just before I headed into the house to get ready, I picked up my neighbor's three-legged cat in our driveway while Demian walked by. The cat recoiled, running her claws down my arm causing a bead of blood to rise and keep rising for the next hour.

By then, it had been eleven years since this little black silky-eared dog had been dropped off on my porch, her former humans speeding off before I could protest that she really wasn't a Golden Retriever/Irish Setter mix. Sitting on the toilet, placing pressure on the long, deep scratch that wouldn't stop bleeding, I talked to Demian about what I hoped was just wedding jitters, normal cold feet, my reluctance to take huge steps. She had known me for a long time, and I appreciated her perspective although I never could understand her grunts and sighs. I figured if no one aggravated her enough for her to bite them, she was okay with the situation.

Fifteen months later, I had a little girl. Demian seemed okay with that, too, if a little indifferent. When Sarah could sit up in the bike trailer with her helmet on, I placed Demian in the back where I swear, I saw her roll her eyes, hold one paw under her chin, slowly shaking her head back and forth like Jack Benny.

We had bought a grand Mountain Avenue two-story home with a carriage house and a deck protected from the sun by towering trees. It was two blocks from City Park with its lake and huge swaths of green space for a kid to run. Unfortunately, it also had stairs unlike the small one level bungalow we were leaving behind.

Demian was twelve years old, and her running days were over. She would never be able to climb the stairs and join us at the foot of my bed where she had slept her entire life. I worried about it and thought about constructing a nice place for her to call her own on the main floor. There would have to be a gate, so she wouldn't attempt the curving staircase with its hardwood floors. I figured she'd cry for a while and I'd acquiesce and come down the stairs, sleeping on the living room couch with her. There was no other way.

The week before we moved, Demian had a stroke while I crawled around the floor with a year-old Sarah. At first, I thought she was being funny in her old age, a characteristic I would never have attributed to her. My neighbor was a vet, and he came right over, administering a shot he'd hope would alleviate lingering effects of the stroke. Or she would die. Pretty much a crap shoot, he said.

She died.

I found her at the bottom of the basement stairs where we had left her, guiltily, because the vet said she might defecate and pee everywhere. I still haven't forgiven myself. Her last night on earth was spent alone, not at the foot of my bed. I blame my ex because he didn't want to have to wake up to a shit-strewn bedroom or kitchen. Ultimately, it was my decision. I should have argued harder.

But Demian was ready and maybe I was, too. She had belonged to a past that spanned too many changes and too many years of uncertainty and fear. Just remembering how irresponsible I was with her care, assuming she would be fine, no matter what decision I was about to make.

There was the time I took a job in Palo Alto in California at IBM for three months and left Demian with Felix in Colorado until I could find a place to live. When he showed up with Demian, my landlord was shocked, expecting a little yapper from my description. I may have said something about her being a cute little Cocker Spaniel.

I once took her on a raft trip with Felix when he was a river guide, and we had a raft and a couple of days between trips. If there was a time Demian ever thought of leaving me, that was probably it. She nearly drowned us all, jumping off the raft and swimming through the cold waters of the Snake River, panicked and disoriented. It took days for her to accept my apology and come to bed with me again.

Then there was the time I left Demian with my sister in Fort Collins when she lived in a trailer. How dumb are we in our late twenties? I was with Jay vacationing in Cape Cod before we married, and left Demian with Kathleen. She had been tying her up to the trailer all day and one day Kathleen decided it was cruel. Demian took off and when I called Kathleen to check in, Demian had been missing a few days.

I couldn't breathe. Kathleen hadn't placed a missing dog ad in the paper (she didn't have the money) and had called the 'pound' once. I called my friend Deni who had a radio show and asked her to tell her audience to be on the lookout for a pretty, black dog with velvety ears and a willingness to eat most anything. I arrived back in Fort Collins two nights later. Around 11:00 p.m. I got a call from the police station downtown.

They said they had my dog, according to her collar, which had a tag with her name, my name, address, and phone number. Demian had been missing five days. I jumped in my Chevy pickup and drove to Laporte Avenue. I was about two blocks from the station when I ran out of gas. It was an older pickup, and it didn't register how much gas I had. Kathleen's boyfriend had used it while I was gone and conveniently forgot to fill it up. I left it parked in front of a local bar, locked it, and ran the two blocks. It was Demian, ragged and thinner, her coat tangled and covered with burrs.

I begged her forgiveness, repeating "I'm sorry, I'm sorry" over and over much to the cops' amusement. I needed a ride and none of them would put this stinky mess of a dog in their patrol cars. Jay hadn't come back with me, so I called an old boyfriend Ray, and he came right over, telling me Demian smelled like she rolled over a skunk and ate it.

Unfortunately, this wasn't long after I had broken up with

Felix. He was drinking at the bar where I had left my car. He never drank, so a couple of beers put him over the edge. He saw my pickup parked there, "On purpose!!!" he raged, thinking I was an asshole and thumbing my relationship with Jay at him. Jay lived about a mile away so in his drunken and confused state, he figured I was being spiteful, basically a horrible person, and laughing at him. He took his Bronco, headed to Jay's house, and revved the car back and forth over the small front lawn, destroying it.

Jay came home the next day. Felix realized the damage he had done the next morning and immediately went back, left a note, and had someone fixing the lawn within the week.

In all of this, I was a jerk, leaving him so abruptly for Jay and not understanding the extent of his feelings and his suffering. I had the empathy of a sociopath. I hated myself.

But I had Demian back and I was never going to leave her with anyone else again.

We're supposed to grow from difficult situations, learning from them and, with any luck, not repeating questionable behavior, but I wondered at the time if there was something wrong with me—I had put my dog in danger and carelessly caused great pain to a long-time partner. I want to believe we all can change. I'm just not sure we do.

Demian was my last dog for seven years—a long time for me. I had a child now and soon would have another. It was all I could handle I suppose. Sometimes I think it was because I didn't deserve another dog. They forgive too easily.

CHAPTER 5
BECCA

1989–2001

I was standing outside Sudbury Valley Shelter, hovering nearby while my kids ran around a dark red, nervous Golden Retriever mix. She's snapping as if chased by a squadron of wasps. Too high-strung, I thought. The shelter employees said she had just come in and they hadn't had time to evaluate her. She was beautiful but flawed. Something was making her crazy and I wanted none of it.

Seven years had passed since Demian died. My husband and I lost our big, beautiful home on Mountain Avenue in Fort

Collins after some questionable financial decisions. We had a toddler, a large mortgage, and no savings.

It all came crashing down. Jay started looking for jobs in both Chicago and Boston. Chicago was his hometown and Needham, right outside Boston, was mine. Mom and a few siblings were spread across the East Coast. I supposed I could learn to drive in Boston traffic.

One winter night I was running my miles around City Park Lake in Fort Collins, angry and cursing my husband in the darkness. We were losing everything. I was so angry at Jay; I was creating scenarios in my mind as to my next steps, each one ended with me leaving him.

Someone I knew called out from the darkness. She must have seen me under the streetlight I had just ran under. I stopped. It was the woman who did Tarot or maybe she was a psychic reader or something. I can't remember now. We chatted for a minute and then she said, "Congratulations!"

For what? I shook my head and shrugged my shoulders. For losing my home? For getting chased out of town? For never seeing my friends again or the running club or bike paths or the Old Town that would blossom into a mecca for the rest of the country?

"You're pregnant!" she beamed at me.

The hell I am.

"It's a boy and he has dark hair and he's big!"

The hell he is.

Anyway, she was wrong. He had blonde hair until he was about twenty. It's a little darker now.

Jay did let me choose where we would move. Boston or Chicago. My family or his. I chose Boston.

Boston had Cape Cod.

I was close to giving birth to Dan. Jay and I spent a long hot New England summer at my mom's condo outside of Boston, sleeping on a foldout couch while Sarah took the small extra bedroom so she could go to bed early. Jay got a job and we moved into a third-floor walk-up in Brookline two weeks before Dan was born. A year later, I got sick of avoiding piles of dog shit on narrow Brookline sidewalks, navigating a stroller and a toddler on our way to a park. I wanted out of the city and into the suburbs where I could run and bike without fear of getting killed. And where there were other kids who played in the streets and ran around the neighborhood playing tag until dusk. I missed the wide streets and bike paths of Fort Collins and the ability to breathe in a bigger sky. We moved to a rental house in Wellesley—five minutes from my hometown of Needham. The older home backed up to Route 9 and was part of a lovely tree-lined neighborhood where kids played in front yards and their moms called them in for dinner every night.

It had been nearly twelve years since I had seen Bruce and fifteen years since he had left Demian and me by the roadside near my house in Fort Collins, Colorado. He had sent me a letter soon after he got home to Boston, professing his love and how he wanted me to come back. It scared me to death. I was convinced he didn't really know how clueless and ridiculous I was, despite spending the bulk of my teen years with me. I never wrote him back.

That Christmas of 1972, I flew home to Boston. I got up the courage to call Bruce, or at least his mother since I didn't have his number. She hesitated when I asked for his phone number at his place near the Museum School. I could feel her discomfort over the phone.

"Well, Bruce is here, visiting us with his girlfriend."

He picked up the phone.

"Hey."

"Hi."

What else was there to say? Everyone was listening on his side of the phone. I imagine the girlfriend, eventually his wife, seated at the kitchen table, pretending to be interested in his mom's tablecloth, smoothing it over and over, while her life collapsed around her. Many years later, I would learn from Bruce the one thing that terrified his wife was me coming home again.

We must have said something to each other, innocuous and stupid, I assume.

We hung up and I walked out to the side porch stairs, calling Taffy to sit with me. I placed a pack of cigarettes beside me and planned to smoke every one of them. I told Taffy it was okay; Bruce would find out soon enough I wasn't 'special' or artsy or funky or whatever I thought he needed. It's crazy to think otherwise, and I would be hurt eventually.

A couple of days later, Bruce showed up at my Mom's house at eight in the morning, jumping on my bed with a handful of snow trying to wake me. Mom had left for work. Nancy was upstairs in the attic. We lay there laughing and eventually made love.

I became 'the other woman.' His girlfriend had left to spend the holidays with her family. We had the week. I came home a couple of times a year for the next three years. Bruce was always there, sometimes showing up at the airport.

When Bruce and his girlfriend married, my mom sent me the invitation three months after it happened, afraid like *The Graduate*, I'd show up at the church, banging on the upstairs window, professing my devotion to Bruce, and begging him to reconsider his choices. If I had known about the wedding, I might've.

And here I was again, years later with a husband and two kids, thinking of Bruce and our screwed-up relationship, living five minutes from where a large part of it had been acted out— our hometown of Needham. My friends, my career, my running paths, my tribe were all back in Colorado. Some of my family lived in the Boston area and it was good to be near Mom, but I needed buddies.

I no longer knew who I was or where my soul had disappeared to—with any luck it was in a place where it was being cared for and comforted because it wasn't in good hands with me. My resentment marinated in a stew of loneliness, disregard, and a nagging fear my life was over. A few months after Dan was born, my husband decided it was best he worked in Washington D.C. all week then come home on weekends and pretend it was enough.

I felt like a hired nanny, not a loved wife and mother. There was a lot wrong with our marriage and we should have had couple's therapy a lot earlier than we did, but we didn't. When Jay was home and we went to his work events or his friend's homes, I sat numb, wishing I could have stayed home. These people had lives, they liked each other, they ran and biked and went on trips together. We were recovering from a bankruptcy, and other than the signatures I brought to my husband to sign for bankruptcy court, he refused to ever talk about it again. If any couple ever needed to talk with a therapist, expose our deep wounds and resentments, it was us.

I didn't know if Bruce had moved away from Needham or had come back to where his parents lived. I looked in the Needham phonebook one day and there he was. It took months, but one hot August afternoon, I ventured up to his house and rang the doorbell. I wish I could go back and figure out what I was thinking, what I thought would happen. I remember picturing his wife and kids and how we would all get along and talk about the old days.

Like the time when Bruce visited me every day in the hospital when I broke my kneecap in high school. Or the times when Bruce picked me up after my shift at Bergson's Soda Shop then drove out to Rosemary Lake where we smoked Marlboros and listened to Van Morrison. The time when he hitchhiked out to Colorado to ask me to come home with him. These are the times I remembered.

He didn't answer, so I left him a note on his front door.

"Hi Bruce, it's Roberts!" the note began.

Why my last name instead of Mary? I thought it would be more casual, indicative of our platonic status (in case he didn't tell his wife about me).

"I'm back! (I didn't know it was his wife's greatest fear.) Long story. Got 2 kids. Call me. Would love to meet your family!" (Not really.) I signed it 'Mary' just in case he was confused about who it was.

He called and asked me to come over. His family was spending the week down the Cape with his wife's parents, and he was working in his shop in the back of his house. I remember what I wore, khaki shorts and a white T-shirt, and that I brought three-year-old Dan with me, who spent the time hanging on to the hem of my shorts. Bruce was standing, holding a drill, and talking to a friend who had stopped by.

His hair was shorter, but he had the same blue eyes and hesitant smile as if he didn't want to look so happy. He later told me his friend commented about me, "She's trouble." It was the first time I wanted to be "trouble," even if it cost me everything.

There is no excuse for an affair. None. Zilch. Nada. I wasn't looking for one, I just wanted to feel alive again and happy. It was as if we had never parted and we spent the next four years bringing misery to our families and ourselves, interrupted by moments of unmitigated happiness. But was it? This is what insanity is—incalculable joy interspersed with a sadness that left me helpless and apologetic to my young kids, now three and seven, who I could barely care for.

I had to do something, so I moved the kids and me out of the Wellesley rental and found a desolate old farmhouse about five miles away. Without my husband. Many years passed before Jay told me he went down to the basement of the Wellesley home and cried when I first told him about Bruce. I wish I had known. I wish I had known my leaving upset him.

When he just agreed to the separation and found himself a place in Cambridge, what I had felt in my heart was confirmed. He didn't love me. Unfortunately, that knowledge, true or not, kept me strong in my determination to not spend the rest of my life with him.

It's why we were standing in front of this shelter for the third time, looking for a dog to keep the monsters at bay for me *and* my kids. The new place sat in the heart of Dover, an enclave of horsey people with blue-blood money a few miles west of Boston. The rundown house where my kids and I moved to was probably the original landowner's house, then relegated to the caretaker, then a sanctuary for separated moms with kids and a dog looking for quiet star-filled nights and a huge yard. No fence unfortunately, so we had to adopt a well-behaved and trained dog who liked kids *and* didn't mind being the center of competition for her affection.

Sarah spotted the dog sitting in her kennel, shaking. We walked her outside. She shook and shied away from our touch like a wild mustang. I exaggerate, of course, but with two young kids, I didn't want to worry about a dog fear-biting. But Sarah had already named this frenetic dog.

"Rebecca!" she shouted. Minutes later, I paid the adoption fee and collected the note her previous owners had left.

"We're too old to take care of her," it said. "She needs a family, someone to walk her and spend time with her." Rebecca was four years old. How the hell old were they four years ago when she was an adorable and pudgy red golden puppy? Did they think she wouldn't grow into the magnificent animal she became, needing exercise, obedience lessons, and a warm human to sleep next to? Or were they just jerks?

Rebecca was Sarah's and she took care of her, feeding, walking, and sleeping soundly by her side. We concocted a story about her past, based on her behavior. Becca walked wide circles around Dan, looked sideways at him and once tried to bite him. She snapped at our feet if we tried to rub her belly with them. She shook uncontrollably when voices were raised. Our made-up story involved an old couple who just wanted a grandchild. Little boys teased her through the chain link fence, her owners were screamers who kicked her when she was in the way. But that's too easy. She was just another dog with issues.

It took some time, but it was on our long runs through rural Dover when Becca and I became friends. She was born to run. We took the dirt path into Noanet Woodlands from Caryl Park right after I dropped off the kids at school on early spring mornings. It smelled like dew, sweet fern, and sugar maple trees. In the summer, it was every berry bush imaginable and milkweed, mustard, orchids, milkwood, nightshade, poppies, clover, trillium and on and on. Long-ago Native Americans cultivated huge amounts of medicinal plants and herbs in these woods. I didn't know its history at the time, but looking back, I see why I fled to this place when I couldn't breathe for the sorrow, when I wanted only the woods to hear my sobs, when my heart shattered. When I didn't know where else to go.

As soon as we left the parking lot, I'd take off Becca's leash and wind it around my waist. She flew, her scrambling among the pine needles and leaves the only sound except the slow steady pounding of my running shoes. She headed straight to the Lower Mill Pond about a mile into our run, checking back to make sure I was still there. My pace quickened, my leg muscles warmed and prepared to follow my dog wherever she wanted to go. I loved this. I loved her.

There was a wildness about her I coveted. She could do this all day but understood that I couldn't. She didn't blame me for it, but I wondered some days if I should just leave her for a time, flying through the trees and searching or maybe just running from whatever scared her as a pup. Despite being a golden retriever mix, Becca was uncomfortable filling the role of a typical pampered American dog, doing our bidding when we want to be amused by our dogs' antics. She tolerated our hugs but was uncomfortable with our affections. She relented with time and maybe even came to enjoy it. I was always careful to ask her permission.

One summer in Peaks Island, Maine, I rented a cottage by the cold Atlantic Ocean for the kids and me and Becca. We had gone to Cape Cod as kids, visiting my uncle's house by the ocean. I wanted my kids to know the sea, too, but the Cape was more than I could afford now. With its rocky beaches and the ocean's Arctic-like temperature, Maine was for the hardy. We walked the island's formidable beaches, not like the warm summer Cape Cod beaches filled with families and ice cream trucks. I liked that it took commitment and fortitude to 'go to the beach' at Peaks Island. It felt like a triumph as we sat with our towels spread over sand littered with large stones poking into our sit bones.

During our stay, we were usually the only ones seeking sun and surf most days so bringing Becca was okay with no complaints about her shooting up and down the beach, sharply turning, kicking up sand, and barking all the way back down to the other side of the cove. At night, it could feel lonely and isolating as the surf pounded the rocks and nothing in the community was open after eight o'clock. Becca and I would sit on the porch and stare out at the dark, listening to a gang of twelve-year old boys tooling around in the black night on their BMX'ers looking for trouble but not quite ready for it. She barked at them.

I thought she was protecting us. Or maybe she wanted to be out there with them, howling in the night, yelling at someone or something, fighting back at a cruel memory. I put my arm around her. She smelled like the sea, salt clinging to the tips of her red coat. I always hosed her off after an ocean swim, but I forgot that day.

I was never a 'dog whisperer.' For the most part, I failed to figure out what the hell any of my dogs wanted. But that night, I felt the tug of a night spent running the beach and the woods. Becca must have felt it too. I thought about letting her out, but the risk of losing her was too great. It was late. I was sleepy. Becca looked at me, yawned and stretched, her front legs bowed before her, her rump in the air. By the time I finished brushing my teeth, Becca was asleep on my bed. I'm grateful the wrench of love and companionship was at least as strong for Becca as the desire to run free.

We had only had her about a year before she tried to take a bite out of Dan. It was a warning bite, no flesh broken, no trip to the ER or house arrest. Dan had sat next to her on the porch. He must have been too loud or moved too quickly, she turned and clamped down on his arm as if scolding a puppy. His sweatshirt took the brunt of her teeth, but he was startled. For a moment, I imagined she was gone from our lives, returned to the shelter with an admonition she couldn't be around kids. Was this when I decided second (and third and fourth) chances would be the rule in our household? I told Dan to be more careful. Becca was staying.

She also didn't like anyone touching her with their feet. Her hackles rose, and she jumped up, giving the offender a dirty look. Sometimes she snapped dangerously close to young toes daring to cross a boundary whose genesis was unknowable but guessable. I swore to Becca I would seek revenge on the previous owners, going back to the Sudbury Valley shelter demanding the miscreants' names. I wouldn't get far. Like some mothers giving up a baby for adoption, owners who surrendered dogs didn't want to be contacted.

I was being unreasonable, and maybe Becca's original humans had experienced a decrease in physical ability. Maybe one of them had had a heart attack or was suffering from

Parkinson's and having the responsibility of a young, intelligent, and athletic dog was too much.

I doubt it, but who am I to judge anyone's poor decisions?

* * *

As the affair with Bruce intensified, Becca and I upped our running mileage and pace. I let her run free through the woods for as long as she wanted. Sometimes I didn't see her for twenty minutes or more. Where did she go and who was she chasing? Or maybe she was outrunning her old life, free and unafraid now, just being a dog. Maybe it's what I was doing, running from every bad decision I had made and every consequence that was about to destroy my family, Bruce's family, and whatever secure future I had bargained for. It didn't free me.

Sometimes Becca would turn and run back toward the parking lot. Most of the time it meant the arrival of a dog she liked, but every so often—it was Bruce. Becca would stop her pell-mell run to nowhere, sniff the air and take off back from where we just came. Bruce knew I spent most mornings in Caryl Woods, and he would appear on the path, Becca beside him, looking like she was escorting him to where I stood, grinning yet fearful we couldn't stop this train wreck. Selfish, stupid, and wrong. Bruce would throw her sticks out into the pond, and we'd act like we were a normal couple out with their dog on a misty spring morning, holding hands and laughing. But we weren't, and we never would be. And we both knew it.

When Jay took the kids for the weekend to his place in Cambridge, it was Becca and me alone in the Dover house, and later Becca and Jesse when we lived in the old Victorian in Natick. I had left behind friends in Colorado and come back to a place I didn't know anymore.

But I ran—a lot. And Becca was right with me, lopping alongside, leash-less but alert to my admonitions to not chase the rabbit, or cross in front of me or my requests to move closer to the shoulder of the road when a bike or car came up behind us. The roads were wide and shady, a relief in the summers but icy in the winters. We didn't care. Mile after mile, we placed one foot, one paw after another, grateful to be here and able to run long and silent and with each other.

Weeks would pass when I wouldn't see Bruce, and those weekends spent alone in a dark house with no lunches or dinners to make, no games or practices to go to and no kids fighting, broke me.

After a persistent injury sidelined my running, I stumbled across Kundalini Yoga, a practice that changed something fundamental in my psyche. I felt powerful and clear and convinced our love could not be denied. We were privileged to experience such heights of love. I began to think of nothing else. It was truly 'Nectar of the Gods' territory. Maybe this was the psychedelic trip we should have taken years ago. Better late than never, I thought.

I cried a lot, waiting for the phone call so we could meet. There were no cell phones then. Sometimes he'd park near my house and just wait for me. I confess I did the same. I grieved all the time while walking the dogs or lying alone at night with them on either side of me when the kids were with their dad. The possibility that I was an idiot terrified me. As it should have.

Bruce stopped by less and less. I knew why but I wanted him to say it, I wanted him to admit he was giving us up, that he couldn't leave his wife. This is a part of my life I want to deny ever happened. Not just because I was foolish, or it was all wrong in every way, but because I never wanted to be vulnerable to anyone or anything and yet I stood, in Noanet Woodlands, hoping Bruce would show up magically and everything would work out. I'd get to know his kids; my kids and dogs would welcome them. How silly of me, how selfish and embarrassing.

We spent nearly two years in that small house in Dover. It was a place to hide and heal, running the Noanet Woodlands and the town's rural back roads, but it was lonely—our little cabin an outpost on twenty acres that the owner used as a horse boarding facility. When the kids were with their dad, I wrote in the living room, Becca by my feet, and listened to the coyotes howling, their way to keep in touch with friends and family. Becca listened, her right ear cocked, her eyes bright and alert. I wondered if she thought she was included in that call to gather.

Becca was steady and generous in her loyalty to me. At home, she barely left my side, even when the kids came home from school. I know Sarah felt it keenly, saying I took Becca from her. I probably did. A year later, I bought a house in Natick, a few miles from Dover. I was happy to leave that place where too much time alone and the call of a wild animal made us question our decisions. Sarah wanted another dog. What could I say? What any guilty, depressed, confused, and sorrowful mother would say. "What's another dog?"

CHAPTER 6
JESSE

1992–2003

I did not want this dog.

I am not fond of black labs with their oily coats and cow-manure-like stink. Sarah's basketball coach had bought two black lab puppies from a local breeder and Sarah was smitten. She came home one day, ready to hand over Becca's allegiance to me (as if she had a choice), if she could have one of these adorable puppies!

What? We were shelter people!

"Let's just go see," she begged.

I would do anything to gain ten-year-old Sarah's love and

admiration even if it lasted only for a car ride home before she turned on me again. Our relationship suffered after our move from Colorado. Dan was born, I left her father, my unhappiness spilled over her like a toxic waterfall. I knew I wasn't a good mom during those years.

I should have been stronger, but as soon as we got to the breeder's home, Sarah fell to her knees madly in love with the runt of the litter. She was tiny and had a turned-out right foot that would only get worse. It all went too fast. The breeder said, "Take her, she's yours," as if such generosity was real. If someone like us didn't take this puppy, she wouldn't be of any use to them and she would be killed. I hated pretending that they were good people, just trying to make everyone happy. Though I think we still paid fifty dollars for her.

Ten minutes later, we were in the old Volvo headed home with a new puppy and a grateful daughter, all temporary, ethereal events, but I basked in the glow of happiness-creator until Jesse threw up in Sarah's lap. For just a split second, I thought Sarah would tell me to turn around and take the dog back, but she didn't. It took me a couple of days to rid the car of its drunken binge stink.

It was a seamless transition for Becca, and she treated the pup gently. Sarah adored Jesse, making the transference of Becca's allegiance to me easier. Becca was officially mine now and she rode with me everywhere in an old Volvo wagon whose flooring in the back was so rusted, I told the kids to never put their feet down. I made Becca sit up front, so she wouldn't mistakenly step on the flooring and be tragically killed in a messy and horrifying car accident.

Jesse grew fast and Becca seemed okay with her new companion, although Becca was still the queen and Jesse the obsequious and looney personal companion.

Unfortunately, I don't remember much of Jesse's time at the

house on Winnemay street in Natick. She played with the neighborhood kids and Sarah did the work of a good dog mom.

And I ran further down the rabbit hole without the ability to turn around. My husband and I were still not divorced. He told me later that he thought I would change my mind about Bruce and come back to him. Instead, I borrowed the down payment for a house in Natick from my brother and my husband put his name on the loan. I now had a garage, a second bathroom and a neighborhood crowded with kids.

When we moved to Natick, it was only a few miles from Dover but the drive back to Noanet took too much time and we sought trails and woods that dotted our new town. It was Becca and Jesse I wrapped my heart around while we sat on the couch late into the night, watching reruns of Seinfeld. I'd wake up late morning, drink two cups of Earl Gray tea then head out for a short walk with both dogs. The long runs in the woods were only with Becca. Lean and athletic, she never strayed from our path, never distracted by other dogs or squirrels, turning left then right with a slight tug on the leash, by my side until we slowed down a block from the house. I don't remember what I did all day, but I remember the conversations I had with Becca, who'd sit attentively listening, her head cocked to one side.

When Jesse was still a little pup, I pulled off the side of the road onto a dirt parking area to take the dogs for a short walk into the woods before heading out to do food shopping. A crisp in the air, the sun barely warm, the ubiquitous pond with the screeching of ducks warning of incoming dogs, the leaves right in between their change—an early fall day in New England.

I love this, I thought. If only it could have been with Bruce, if only I hadn't been so scared, if only... and there I was, investigating the tunnels and holes that define a rabbit warren. I had Jesse by the leash since she had no sense at all about ducks or cars or strangers. A man was striding quickly toward us. Becca, by the edge of the pond, her eyes on the ducks, lifted her head and turned towards Jesse and me. Then she spotted him and ran. For a moment I thought we were in trouble, that this guy had seen us pull of the road and was intent on harm. He was too anxious, too focused on our little tribe.

"Heel, Jesse, heel," I shouted, pulling on Jesse's leash, attempting to show the intruder that this may be a pup, but she is vicious, and I must struggle to keep her from tearing you from limb to limb. I looked ridiculous. Jesse wagged her thick, feathery tail and smiled at the guy.

It was Bruce. I hadn't seen him in months.

I let go of Jesse's leash and she yelped and jumped up on his legs while Becca stood by barking and wagging her tail in greeting.

"Another dog, eh?" He grinned at me. "Saw your car, I've been looking for you."

For what reason, I wondered? There had been no formal declaration of closure, no tearful goodbye. Just an unrelenting pain every single day. But still I thought, maybe there's still a chance. Maybe he was at a job site in another state. Maybe he was preparing his family for the disruption in their lives. Maybe, he was slowly devising a plan and he would come to me with it, happy and sure we were doing the right thing.

It turns out that he felt guilty and had re-doubled his effort as good husband and father, but he couldn't do it anymore and had come looking for me. He said he tried to forget about me, he tried to convince himself his wife and kids and life were good and enough, and we'd all be better off. My heart leapt, but for a moment, I wish he had never come looking for me. Every time I saw him, it just prolonged the inevitable. We both knew he would never leave.

Later that day, I would go over each word he said to me, analyzing for the possibility of different meanings, maybe he meant one thing and I heard another. *That's the life of a woman in love with a married man, and I'm no different.* I wrote that in my journal, but never really believed it. I thought I was different, having been in love with Bruce since I was fifteen years old. There was no justification for what I was doing, only the regret and sorrow of someone in an unhappy marriage.

Jesse splashed around in a mud puddle while Bruce and I held each other, leaning against an old oak tree that lent its wide trunk to us. He couldn't stay long but promised to try and get away over the weekend. I knew he wouldn't. That night I allowed Jesse onto the couch, dried mud and leaves and the bodies of dead insects flaking off her, and hugged both dogs, one on either side, grateful for them both.

He called one night and said he couldn't take it any longer; he would tell his wife that night. I taught class in a fog the next morning, rushing home to hear what happened. No phone call for a couple of days. My kids don't know much about any of this. I want to be old enough to not care about what they think about my behavior when they read this, but I think that only comes with death. Bruce called, and by the tone of his voice I knew it was over. Rebecca and Jesse sat next to me on the couch as I listened.

"Kyle broke his arm the night I was going to tell her. He was riding home on his bike and he fell. It was a bad break and he had to go to surgery." Bruce recounted the night.

I stayed silent, knowing what this meant.

"I can't do it, Mary. My family needs me." Bruce cried.

This must be what it feels like when someone has COPD. Or asthma. Can't catch a breath enough to speak or sob or move. I'm sure I wept, then yelled at him when I found the oxygen to do so.

It wasn't long before Bruce came to my house to say goodbye.

Jesse and Becca sat on the couch and watched the two of us try and make sense of the past thirty years. How were we not together? Where were the missteps? How could we have let each other go?

Bruce had started smoking again when we started our affair. I'd bum one off him, despite being a yoga instructor and long-distance runner. It's how we first bonded back in high school, sneaking out behind the school and lighting up. When it looked like we might be together soon, I told him smoking was who we were, not who we're going to be. Maybe he'd start running with me or take up meditation. But we didn't talk about how this would all work, where we'd live, money, kids, alimony, custody. If we had, our affair might have ended long before.

He pulled out his pack and pointed his chin toward the back yard. Both dogs followed us out and sat with us on the grass as Bruce and I lit up. I still wanted answers but what difference would it make anymore? We smoked slowly, knowing that once the cigarettes were out, he would leave.

I walked him to the driveway, remembering the time twenty years ago that my dog Demian and I had walked him to the road where he would hitchhike back to Boston. This time, he didn't need a ride. Bruce got in his Nissan pickup, filled with the tools of his trade as a carpenter and sculptor, and backed out of the driveway. I watched the truck move down the street, slowly picking up speed, just like I did so long ago. This time I had two dogs, one on either side of me, sitting quietly, but I didn't cry. I chose not to believe he was gone forever.

There was a lesson to be learned here but I refused it.

Before he left, Bruce told me to go back to my husband. How could I? This is what I wanted! Passion yet familiarity, feverish sex, acceptance, support, loyalty, affection. Yes, except for the sex, it sounded like I needed another dog.

CHAPTER 7

JAKE

1998–2001

I t was another three years before I woke up one morning, having dreamt about the bike paths in Fort Collins, Colorado, and decided to leave. I put up a vision board with photos of Colorado and me and the dogs running the Poudre Trail with a long leash for Jesse who lagged behind Becca and me. I drew a wandering blue curve for the Poudre River and both my kids on bikes laden with soccer balls, skateboards, rollerblades, and riding off with friends.

My husband and I still weren't divorced, and I told him that I wouldn't leave unless he got a job he would be happy with in

Colorado. I wasn't about to take his kids from him. He got a fantastic assignment, but it meant he would be gone for months, most of the time in Antarctica.

Dan, Jay and I flew to Colorado on a hot July day in 1996. Now thirteen-years-old, Sarah stayed behind to attend a basketball camp with actual WNBA players and coaches at Tufts University. The dogs were in crates in the bottom of the plane and I was convinced they'd be dead when we finally landed. I swear I heard Jesse howling in pain or loneliness or fear. *I'm here, Jesse, don't worry!* I told the luggage handlers to put the Jesse next to Becca, but I imagine they laughed at me after I walked away.

I ran to baggage claim and hurriedly unlatched their crate doors, apologizing the whole time. *I'm so sorry, I'm so sorry!* A faint scent of pee and poo intrudes a bit into this memory right now. Who could blame them?

Jesse had turned into a hefty dog, unable to run the thirty or so weekly miles that Becca and I shared. I wanted to pick her up and cradle her like I used to. Instead, I sat on the dirty linoleum floor of the baggage claim area and hugged her tight. She leaned so heavily into me I rolled back, and we lay there for a moment, her head on my chest, reassuring each other, both needing the long, comforting assurance that we made the right decision.

Our house backed up to an open space area that would periodically flood, and we'd take out a kayak or a boogie board meant for the beaches and paddle around. Jesse loved that, especially after an intense summer downfall that would leave us three to four inches of rain in a couple of hours and slow the drainage. She'd head out back and lie down in the water and watch the rest of us float by in whatever contraption we could find that didn't sink. She'd do that when we moved to the Lake Sherwood neighborhood, yards from a scummy large pond that I thought was a lot cleaner when I bought the house. While

Becca chased the ball into the water or down the cul-de-sac, Jesse had no interest and would lie down, then roll over, trolling for belly rubs.

Dan wanted his own dog, just like his sister had Jesse and I had Becca. That would be three, approaching the slippery slope of 'crazy dog lady' territory. I knew the dogs would be mine when everyone left for college. I hesitated. Then I read about these cool dogs called 'rat terriers' and saw a couple on the bike path the next day.

"That's it," I told Dan. "This should be your new dog! He's feisty, funny, and you could teach him to run next to you on your skateboard and maybe even sail with you on the lake!"

I wanted to make Dan happy. His Dad now lived in Denver and traveled for weeks at a time. I guess I'm to blame for the arrangement. It was my decision to move back to Colorado but only if their dad could get a job in the state. His company had partnered with a business in Colorado, providing logistics and planning expertise for scientific research in the Antarctic.

He got the job, but it also meant trips across the world. Dan was ten years old and no longer my sidekick or as Sarah called him, "Mama's boy." Dan was a handsome boy with long blonde hair and blue eyes who played soccer, skateboarded, and had his left ear pierced at least twice and maybe three times. He had to take each earring out for all his soccer games. He liked his hair long and the name on the back of his soccer shirt had his last name, "April," and I'm sure onlookers thought he was a girl.

My separation from his dad hurt him more than I acknowledged. But if anything could cure unhappiness, it would be a dog, especially his own dog.

I don't why I focused on a small dog, especially a terrier. We were a big dog family and not temperamentally equipped to handle a dog that spent hours thinking up ways to ruin our lives.

Once again, I violated my 'rescue dog' only rule and found an ad in the local paper.

"Hobby breeder on small farm has adorable rat terriers ready for purchase. Raised in home with kids and other animals. Parents on site."

Sounded good to me. Dan was home sick the next day but not sick enough to turn down a puppy all his own. Dan and I went over to the farm about ten miles away and sat on the kitchen floor with ten rat terrier puppies from two different litters. The moms each had a corner of the room and came over to sniff us to make sure we knew what to do with their babies. I was nervous they'd figure out we were terrier newbies and would find a way to communicate their disapproval to their human.

In my imagination, the dogs' owner would point her finger towards the back door, "I'm sorry, but Trixie thinks you are clueless when it comes to caring for these unique dogs so, just move along, please." And we would slink out.

The scene played out in my mind until Dan picked the littlest squirmiest thing, not even four pounds, stark white with two blotches of black on either side of his tiny body and two caramel dots over his eyebrows that looked the candy Boston Baked Beans. Dan sat cross-legged on the yellowing linoleum floor, his hands engulfing the puppy's body, his eyes closed and murmuring sweet things in the puppy's ear.

The owners smiled, and I knew the puppy was ours. There was talk about having to wait a little longer before the pups could leave their mommy at eight weeks, which was okay with me. "We'll come back when he's bigger," I said, offering to leave a deposit. He was the runt, and he needed more mommy time.

"Oh, just take him," the owners held her hands up in the air, in a gesture that said, "Too many little squirts around here!" Dan and I looked at each other, hoping the other had something intelligent to say other than, "We'll take him!" We didn't, and we took him. I should have left him to learn a few more valuable lessons from his Mom and Dad and siblings.

We named him Jake. When the carnage began a few months later, I would revisit this decision and wonder if there was some rite of passage where he would learn how to behave in the human world. Jake missed this and it was our fault.

Jake tussled with the big dogs and they were tolerant, though Becca less so. She had entered the stage of 'Grande Dame' and didn't give a shit anymore except when it came to food and dignified walks. I have photos of Jesse lying down while Jake curled into the expanse of her belly. There's also one where all three dogs occupy the cordovan leather couch Jake would eventually destroy, and Becca sits regally, her eyes rolled up, considering some distant scenario where terriers didn't exist. Jesse is lying down staring into the camera while a ten-pound Jake is in mid jump off the couch. Camaraderie is not the first word that comes to mind when one looks at the photograph.

When Dan was at school, I'd scoop up Jake and nuzzle him, pulling my head back just in time before his sharp little baby teeth dug into my face. We ran together, not far, but fast and he'd leap with joy. But it was like having a sociopath as a pet— we never knew what would make him fly into a fit of rage. Or who he would consider his family at the moment. Humans diagnosed with the disorder appear disturbed, and their acts of mayhem are equally disorganized and spontaneous. The morning he killed all the koi in the backyard pond I had gone out back to pick up dog poop, and the patio was strewn with fish guts, blood, and the remnants of the lily pads. Five minutes earlier he was sitting in my lap, nuzzling my neck before jumping off to investigate something outside.

Jake looked like a madman, his eyes shining, his body smeared in blood and his face commandeered by a sneer which stopped me from moving forward to discipline him. I couldn't back down; it would mean he had won. Every dog trainer will tell you this, but I still worried any aggression toward him would put him over the edge and we would lose him forever. The hose and spigot were within reach and I slowly ratcheted the handle to the right, while reaching for the hose. Jake didn't move. I aimed the hose at him but at the last minute, pointed it to the detritus staining my flagstones. He turned away, licking his chops, and settled down among the new mulch hugging the fence line, making him smell like a winter forest. I let him relax before scooping him up for a soapy bath in the kitchen sink.

One day after a run, I noticed his chest was a light pink and tried to remember what part of the path had reddish dirt. Jake was alert but subdued. I ran him over to my vet down the street. She asked me if I had put out rat poison lately. Never! I declared. No dog owner would do something stupid like that, especially if they had terriers, born with the instinct to rout out things they shouldn't. Yet, the lining around his lungs was bleeding from rat poison.

"Let him die in peace, Mary," my vet said.

Stunned, I said no, and left.

I called Sunny, a healer friend, and she came over with fresh greens, clove oil, and plastic syringes after being assured I had a high-end blender. We juiced everything and squirted it down Jake's throat for five days, doing the same with as much water as he would take. The goal was to inundate his system with Vitamin K, a coagulant that would slow the bleeding. The kids and I took turns holding him close to our bodies and walking and singing for him. Well, I sang, anyway. "You Are My Sunshine" worked best.

Keith was a new man in my life and as much as I'd like to now toss invectives and insults his way, he was helpful. My new job as a real estate agent forced me to leave the house every so often and Keith would take over Jake's care while I was out showing property to clients who babbled on about house prices while I prepared to go home to a dead dog.

Jake didn't respond for five days, but he didn't die either. I fell in love during those days—with Jake, not Keith. Jake needed me to survive. It was my decision to not let him die and to spend my days covered in green slime, smelling like hot mulled cider from the hourly dose of cloves. He ate nothing and barely peed and never pooped. No one thought he would survive. He slept soundlessly all day in my arms while I talked on the phone, whispering so as not to wake him. Dan ran home from school every day, bursting into the house to see how Jake was doing, terrified this was the day he died. He didn't skateboard, or hang with his friends, or go to soccer practice. He rocked him like a baby and squirted green juice down his throat while he ate dinner and did his homework. Recently, I found a notebook a thirteen-year-old Dan wrote about our dogs a few months after Jake recovered.

"I can't imagine not having dogs in my life. Sometimes they are a big pain, especially when they roll in something smelly or throw up in the house, but it would be too boring and quiet without them. I can't imagine what it would be like to not have big Jesse on my bed or Jake not ripping my socks to little pieces. I would miss Becca's smile and how she greets me every day when I come home from school. If I didn't have them it would be like missing part of my family."

A week later, on one of my attempts to get him to walk outside and pee, Jake wandered over to a shrub and peed long and green into the mulch. I swear I heard him sigh, relieved of the confusion and pain of the last seven days.

He was back. I cried. Years later, I read what I should have done at the time: get a thirty-day prescription to Vitamin K1, have him re-evaluated for any lingering issues, or even have an immediate blood transfusion. When I look back, I wonder if I should've just put him out of his misery and maybe ours.

At first, I thought Jake was rambunctious because he was a terrier. Our family was used to golden retrievers and labs—big, goofy dogs whose life ambition is to chase balls, eat, and take up half the bed. When we first got Jake, he'd tear around the house, barking at the other dogs, shadows, and miller moths which he ate with gusto. Then he'd fall asleep in my arms looking so small and defenseless; his little legs quivering from a dream, little brown baked bean spots just above his eyebrows. I was smitten.

But within a year or so, we had signs on the front door, "Enter with care. We have a crazy terrier. Don't look him in the eye." We protected our food with one arm encircling the plate and the other eating defensively with an elbow cocked in the direction of Jake, prepared to knock him in the nose if necessary. I'd scan the counters, looking for a misplaced banana or protein bar left carelessly unguarded, while Jake watched me.

During his short life, Jake destroyed all our leather furniture. He killed every pretty little garter snake daring to enter his territory. One Thanksgiving, he hauled a cooked, glistening turkey out the doggie door, leaving pools of fat and stuffing steaming on the kitchen floor. He shredded all of Dan's socks and peed on his clean laundry and chased his friends down the cul-de-sac. He'd race out the door and down the street, scaring little kids. We had to use childproof locks for the cabinets because Jake could open anything.

Jake slept under my bed. My other dogs would get up and leave the room as soon as he sauntered in. I didn't care. Sometimes I would wake before daybreak and feel his sleeping body unexpectedly nestled in the crook of my arm, his face inches away from mine, and his breath still like a puppy. I'd slide slowly backwards off the bed so as not to wake him. I knew I shouldn't be afraid of my own dog, but I was.

By the time Jake was two years old, our runs on the bike path had become arduous. He challenged every dog regardless of size or temperament. I'd pick him up and throw him over my shoulder while he yapped fiercely at the other dogs. I kept running, repeating, "Sorry, sorry, sorry," to everyone, hoping they'd understand the burden of loving an unlovable dog. Jake would sit on the back porch late at night and wail. It was a sound so unnerving; I'd lock him in my bedroom and throw a blanket over his head. People told me it sounded like the cry of a wounded wild animal.

I was a mother protecting her child. He was broken, and I couldn't fix him, but neither could I give up. Most of my other dogs have been and will always be rescues, some with serious issues, but they've never made me re-think how to enter a room.

* * *

I didn't recognize the signs of painful arthritis with Becca. Dogs don't show pain if it means no more long walks or throwing the ball or going upstairs to sleep in someone's bed. There's a lot I didn't recognize at the time. I promised myself I would ... next time. Next time, when one of my dogs was suffering but still eager to walk or fetch a ball or climb the stairs. Next time, when they stopped eating, or couldn't poop, or chose to sleep in the closet or in their own bed instead of mine, unable to jump on my bed or even navigate the doggie stairs I finally bought.

Becca was the queen, the epitome of elegance and discernment; she had been my companion through the deepest sorrow I had ever succumbed to, she had run hundreds of miles with me and spent years by my side, steady and watchful, as if I needed her physical presence to acknowledge my existence. I was not going to let her die until I had to.

Dan had begged me not to do it, it wasn't time yet, Becca could still walk and smile and sit on the couch with us, eating the treats shoved deep in our pockets. I tried to explain she was in pain and unable to get up any more without assistance. What was I to do? He took her out to the cul-de-sac and showed me she could walk fine; she wasn't in pain and we were all wrong. He was in high school, and Sarah was leaving soon for college. I didn't want this to be the moment he turned from his mother, disappointed, shaking his head as if he was never going to trust me again.

The vet had already pulled up to our house, carrying her bag of sleep up to the front door. She watched as Dan walked Becca round and round the cul-de-sac, until Becca stopped and swayed a bit, slowly allowing her rear legs to collapse under her. Dan picked her up and walked back in the house, Becca looking small and frail in his arms, her eyes closed. I assumed it was in gratitude.

For just a moment, I wanted to call Bruce and tell him the dog we had walked together in the woodlands, who had run back to the parking lot to escort him to the pond where I stood waiting, who had fetched the sticks he threw in the pond, who stood by as we kissed and cried in each other's arms, had died at fourteen. It's not that I believed Becca was my consolation prize for not having Bruce in my life. But she was there by my side, always looking at me to make sure I was okay.

I'll take it. Months later when we went back east to visit Mom, we spread her ashes in Noanet Woodlands in Dover. I was happy to set her free.

CHAPTER 8

SADIE

2001–2017

I didn't tell Sadie's origin story for many years. I was embarrassed, having portrayed myself as a hardline animal activist who had occasionally thought about breaking into pet stores, rescuing every pup, spraying graffiti all over the store, accusing them of abuse and neglect, then running into the night with a team of accomplices pulling a wagon full of pups and two or three terrified puppies under each arm.

This was worse than retail therapy—this was dog therapy in a retail environment. I went to a pet store—not on purpose, but impulsively and stupidly.

Sarah was leaving for college on Monday. I hoped we'd get through the next few days without a blow up. I could never write a book about my relationship with my kids. It would probably kill me. So much I did wrong! But I plodded on. Years later, I thought maybe I should've been more involved in Sarah's decision to play soccer at the University of Idaho. But she resisted me, and I didn't insist on her listening to me. I didn't want her to go there because it was Idaho and bereft of liberals. Too many lunatic survivalists. But we had struggled for years as mother and daughter. As much as I thought I was an inept dog mom, I was a much less capable human mom.

After a long day at work, I still needed to get her extra-long twin bed sheets, towels, and other necessities of college life. Keith went with me, and we passed the pet store in the mall on the way to Mervyn's. Becca had died a few months ago and it felt empty at home with just two dogs, Jesse and Jake—one old and crippled and the other, well, insane would be a good description and you'd understand if you read the previous chapter.

Honestly, I hadn't yet delved into the dark and sordid world of puppy mills. I just had a vague notion pet stores were evil on some sliding scale level, and we should always rescue. I had already broken the rule twice, so that slippery slope had already been slid down, climbed back up and slid down again.

I stood looking at the poor pups, sniffling and looking sad and disheveled. Two toy fox terriers lay listless in their crate, eye crap streaming from their eyes, their puppiness having abandoned them too early in their young lives.

"Aren't they just the cutest things?" The pet store salesgirl was in high school, her first job most likely, and too skinny and perky. I wanted to slap her and say something about the dogs' condition and wasn't their health her responsibility? She asked me if I wanted to see them. I pointed at the female. We sat in the 'get to know you room' and the sickly pup walked a few steps then settled down to stare at me. Great, I thought, she'll be dead in a week. The dogs were discounted by fifty percent and I wanted both. The male was her brother. I didn't trust Jake, being the arrogant male dog in the house, and assumed he would try and kill another male dog. But it was because of Jake I even considered another terrier. None of this makes sense. Jake was the worst dog I ever had yet I was five minutes from getting a similar dog.

Love is complicated.

Maybe this pup would temper Jake's insanity, maybe he'd settle down and become like the dignified yet mischievous Eddie on *Frasier*, and the two would walk companionably with me along the Poudre Trail, occasionally chasing a rabbit or cooling off along the Poudre River's edge.

I turned to Keith and asked, "Is this crazy?"

I had a habit of asking guys for advice and immediately dismissing everything they said. I have no idea what Keith said to me in response.

I took the sad-looking pup home. I may or may not have remembered the sheets.

Sarah was upset I had brought home this tiny dog just a couple of days before she left for college. I let her name her and she came up with Sadie. A week later, an aging and cranky Jesse was laying on the landing halfway up the stairs, impeding everyone from coming or going. We had to step over her carefully. I didn't think she'd bite any of us, but I wasn't sure she wouldn't.

Unfortunately, little Sadie, at around three pounds, irritated Jesse as Sadie climbed the stairs and that old bit her right on the muzzle, as canine mothers are apt to do to correct their pups. Blood spurted from her muzzle straight up in the air. I assumed she would be dead in minutes having struck a crucial blood vessel that would somehow prevent oxygen from getting to her brain or blood to her heart. All crazy thinking. She was calm. I rushed her to my vet who irrigated the wound and said she'd be fine. In my defense, I never did take anatomy.

A few months later, I found Sadie high up in one of the cottonwood trees listing forward into Lake Sherwood, in a staring contest with a squirrel who was wondering who this creature was and why did she keep following him. Or maybe the squirrel was calling its posse to surround the interloper and throw her off the branch to her inevitable death. I screamed at her and she reluctantly turned a graceful pirouette and came down. This behavior would continue for the next few years, climbing any tree that offered her a welcoming branch bent gracefully toward the earth, a hand-up as it were, for my little girl to race up the tree's trunk, overseeing her land, her kingdom.

* * *

Jake's obsession with rocks was the thing that finally killed him. My kids would bring their friends over, give Jake a rock about ten inches across, weighing about two pounds and watch him as he scraped and clawed at it, whining in increasing decibels. They'd all laugh until I stopped it. Was he frustrated it was too big for him to pick up and carry down to the lake? Did he think it was a toy and it didn't squeak, and it pissed him off?

A ball didn't get his attention, but a rock did, and Keith and Dan would throw them high and far for Jake to pursue. I finally forbid the practice when Jake could run faster and jump higher than any one of us thought possible.

We had just celebrated Jake's third birthday when Dan and I drove to watch Sarah play soccer at college.

The day we left I warned Keith. "No more rocks for Jake. He's too good now. First thing you know he'll catch it and that will be the end of him. I mean it, Keith."

I felt like a bitchy mom with a recalcitrant son who never

took me seriously. Keith was younger by thirteen years and I suspected him of all kinds of deceptions, but right now I needed him to pay attention to me. Sure, I should have left him years before or never took up with him in the first place. But I needed help with two near teens, too many dogs and a new career. He was handsome, we had been friends in Boston, a fellow yogi, and I thought we had a decent arrangement. He could live with us in exchange for him not being a dick and helping with an occasional dinner and with Dan, my son who had lived most his life surrounded by demanding females.

It sounds callous. It didn't start out like that but it's where we were now. And all I cared about were my dogs who were being left in the care of a guy who didn't give a shit, so, yes, I blame myself for Jake's demise.

We were gone only four days, but when we got back, Jake was not himself. He didn't even protest when I held him and rubbed his little nub of a tail, humming "You Are My Sunshine" in his ear. We took him to his last obedience class, and he did what he was asked, if unenthusiastically. It was my first clue something was wrong—he never did anything I asked.

The next day, Jake was in the vet's operating room, a rock lodged in his small intestine. I brought him home after a couple of days in recovery, but he wasn't the same. I thought the drugs were making him meek and docile, but, no, drugs wouldn't do this to him. He was dying.

My vet, Dr. Elayne, takes me back to see Jake. He is lying on the OR table, the endotracheal tube still in his mouth, keeping him alive. She tells me I can pet him while I wait for my son to arrive.

Instead, I crawl onto the operating table and envelope him in my arms. He's warm, asleep maybe. Burying my face in his neck, I cry. I beg him not to go.

My son Dan is standing in the doorway when I get up. It's his birthday. I start to say something about it being a lousy one, but Dan's eyes close and he exhales. He's not sad. He's relieved. I understand. Jake was a difficult dog.

In the days to come, neighbors would stop me and express their condolences as I ran solo along the path behind my house. I thanked them quickly and moved on before I started crying. A friend told me the news of the 'Devil Dog's' demise has raced up and down the tidy streets of our Parkwood East neighborhood. Devil Dog! I had no idea! I told my friend I was called The Witch of May Street when I was a kid. Two peas in a pod, I said. She touched my arm and said, "You did your best, Mary."

Did I? Was Jake legitimately crazy or did I just not pursue the knowledge or resources to help him? He needed an evaluation from a good trainer and then training, maybe even Cesar Milan's Dog Psychology Center, but then I heard about his techniques and I was afraid Jake would come back cowed and his spirit broken. I could attend Victoria Stillwell's Academy and spend seven thousand dollars to become the ultimate dog trainer. Or I could take him to classes, which I did, but they never quite took hold, like an incorrigible first-grader who uses his adorableness to please his teacher but hurls little Jimmy off the jungle gym when the playground monitor's back is turned. A terrifying Eddie Haskell.

I can't help but think his early separation from his canine mommy was the cause of his instability and destructive personality. Or maybe the rat poison had altered his brain chemistry just enough it turned him into a Frankenstein's monster. All we knew was if he stared at you for too long, sitting across the room, you'd better get up and run for your life.

* * *

Sadie held her ground with all dogs, chasing them off the beach around the lake, having established it as her territory. If small garter snakes found their way in our backyard, she'd kill them with extreme efficiency, having learned the skill from Jake who only lived a couple of months after I brought Sadie home. As much as I still mourned the loss of Devil Dog Jake, I'm grateful he didn't have more time to educate her in the ways of his Gang of One. They would have been a formidable pair and I'm certain, they would have been in doggie jail within the year.

It was after Jake's death, but it couldn't have been too long after. I was out in Idaho again with my daughter, watching her play another game. I had left Sadie with Keith, reluctantly, but she was too young to be boarded and he still lived with us and she was just a little thing. How hard could that be?

I don't understand the connection between me, my dogs, and any relationship I've ever had with a man. It's amorphous and confusing and anytime I try to poke it, it pokes back, refusing to answer even a simple inquiry—why can't you accept my unreasonable attachment to dogs? One may have nothing to do with the other, but I doubt it. Keith was no different. He may have tried to fit in with all the animals who wandered through our lives, though I suspected he didn't care about them and it was all an act.

When Keith called me on Sunday morning while I was on a run on the Moscow, Idaho bike trails to tell me he lost Sadie, I wanted to kill him.

"I must not have closed the front door all the way," he reasoned.

What? Who doesn't close the front door unless they're in a hurry? Or stupid and careless. Our front door would sometimes sway open with a stiff wind off the lake if it we didn't take the time to make sure it was closed properly. I didn't put the pieces together for a few years. He had been having an affair and either he invited her to our bed, or he was in a hurry to meet her in some deserted parking lot.

And he forgot about my girl Sadie. I should have kicked him out when Jake died, knowing he caused his death despite his denial.

We hadn't been the same since. I didn't know about the affair, but I knew something was wrong. His behavior around pretty—and younger—women was irritating, but he dismissed my concerns with a shake of his head and a practiced sigh. Gaslighting hadn't been a part of my lexicon up to then. I thought I needed therapy for my trust issues. Then I thought he didn't like my dogs, and he didn't know how to tell me. Come to find out, it wasn't my dogs he didn't like, it was me.

Sadie had spent the morning wandering around the lake when a neighbor found her without a collar or tags. I blame Keith, though I have no evidence he removed her collar and tags. She was microchipped, but it didn't help. My neighbor brought her home to his wife and they decided to call Larimer Humane Society and have her picked up. A week prior, I had taught Kundalini Yoga in the community room for the neighborhood and the wife had been there. Sadie also attended and had wandered around the room for a bit then lay down for a long nap. It didn't click for this woman this was the same dog she had met five days ago. Months after this incident, I mentioned it to the woman, but she seemed uncomfortable and I dropped it. Reluctantly.

The story I got from Keith was filled with holes and improbabilities. He had forgotten my long history with shelters, dogs getting picked up, and my knowledge of how Larimer Humane works. He told me he called Larimer Humane and asked about a dog like Sadie and they said they hadn't picked any dog up in our neighborhood with a similar description except for a min pin.

Sadie looked exactly like a min pin, a miniature pinscher, a tiny version of a Doberman, though they aren't the same breed. He said he described Sadie to them, who had the exact coloring as most min pins. I accept Keith didn't know his dog breeds, but shouldn't the folks at the shelter know something about dog breeds? And why didn't you go down to the shelter, Keith, just three miles from the house and check it out?

I asked him again and again when he picked me up from the airport Sunday night.

"Why, Keith? Why did you just sit on your ass and not check it out? Of course, she was talking about Sadie, and she's been there for thirty-six hours alone and afraid!" I even kicked his glove box I was so furious.

"And why didn't you go down this morning? They're open all weekend!"

He said they led him to believe they weren't open on Sundays. Led him to believe? What's unbelievable is I didn't throw his clothes off the balcony when we got home and slam the door in his face.

In the middle of my rant, Keith got a call from the neighbor who had found Sadie and called Larimer Humane on Saturday morning. I grabbed the phone. The guy was sorry for not recognizing my dog. Keith had gone around the neighborhood Sunday putting flyers in people's mailboxes with Sadie's picture and his phone number. I yelled at him for that, too.

"Who opens their mailboxes on a Sunday? Why didn't you just leave it tucked into their screen doors? Or peeking out from under their door mats?"

It was a long and belittling outburst and to his credit Keith didn't say anything. Later, I thought he was being kind allowing me to get through the possibility of losing one of my dogs. Much later I realized he was out with this other woman and what could he say?

As luck would have it, the neighbor had decided to paint his mailbox Sunday afternoon and found the flyer. He had called immediately. He was apologetic and now remembered whose dog it was. I thanked him and ordered Keith to drive straight to Larimer Humane. We were too late. It had been closed for a while but there was a caretaker. I begged her to let me come in and get my dog. She did go back and check to make sure she was there.

"She's sharing a cage with an older larger dog, but she seems okay."

I was crying by then, more than hysterical and started yelling.

"She's microchipped! Why didn't anyone call me?"

The poor gal didn't know. We went home.

We were there the moment the place opened the next morning. I demanded my dog and to know why they didn't call me. There was some muttered excuse about the microchip machine must not have worked or her chip was placed improperly. I demanded they scan her right then for the chip. It beeped loud and clear. I also questioned their knowledge of dog breeds and how they should have known a min pin and a toy fox terrier could have been easily mistaken for each other. I sensed they were going to call the police or at least some hefty animal control officer who would firmly escort me out the door.

Larimer Humane wanted sixty dollars a day for her boarding which included Saturday, Sunday, and all of Monday though it was only ten in the morning. I told them it was their fault and if they had scanned it correctly, none of this would have happened. I told them I was going to take my dog, go sit in the car and Keith and the front desk could work out how much was owed, and he would pay.

We didn't speak on the way home. He moved out soon after. One day, soon after Keith left, I woke up to my little girl sleeping soundly at the foot of the bed and it made me happier than any time I had been with Keith in the last six years.

CHAPTER 9
TOBY

2001–2012

Sarah came home for Christmas during her first year in college. We were at Walmart, picking up stuff for her second semester at college, her Christmas vacation almost over. Sarah noticed a man holding two puppies under his arms and grinning at a couple of little kids who stood next to him, petting the pups excitedly, looking back at their parents, full of hope for a Christmas puppy.

Sarah was not a little kid, but she went over and picked up a fur ball, brown and black, huge brown eyes, dead ringer for a bear cub.

"Only fifty dollars," the guy said to me. Yeah, fifty dollars and a lifetime of health problems, I thought to myself. Backyard breeders know nothing about genetics and pass on issues that cost clueless puppy owners a fortune.

But Jake had just died, Sadie was a young pup, only a few months old, and Jesse, my old fart of a lab was still around, cranky, and slow, sleeping twenty hours a day and not much trouble. It did seem lonelier at the house with just Sadie skittering across the Saltillo tile. Three dogs had become the norm for our household, possibly in an unconscious attempt to satisfy the universe's need to make me insane or maintain an equilibrium that I didn't understand.

The Feng Shui Rule of Three:

Odd numbers expand and create more energy, even numbers contract and condense. According to feng shui rules, it would have made more sense to have less than three dogs, so I don't know what I was reading to be convinced I *needed* three dogs. I may have misread.

I rationalized that this puppy and Sadie would grow up together in the next few months, rollicking puppies who could cheer up a household devastated by the loss of the crazy but beloved Jake. We had plenty of dog beds, food bowls and even puppy food, so I handed the guy fifty dollars and we left with another puppy-breath sentient being, soon growing into a proud and handsome protector of the hearth and of Sarah. But he would spend the next six months with me and Dan and my two dogs, while Sarah lived in the dorms for the next semester, calling every day, anxious for any news or humorous anecdotes about her first dog—or the first one her mother wouldn't steal. She named him Toby.

On the one hand, it was nice to know that my daughter trusted me with her new puppy. To raise and train him for the next six months, subjecting him to the bad habits and attitudes of my other dogs. On the other hand, I didn't want another puppy.

* * *

There are certain dogs that are simply good dogs, not trained or talented in any realm at all, but gentle to kids and the ignorant. They come when called most of the time. They'll lie beside you, either spine to spine or enveloped in a long bear hug without moving away. Occasionally, they'll snap at the dog sitting next to them if a piece of food has been introduced into the situation but it's rare and a source of amusement. Anytime, day or night, (if they've had dinner), a good dog will comfort you, sighing with you, licking your face occasionally, and settle in for a good cry with you when required.

This was Jesse. I remember her with gratitude and affection, especially after the last fifteen years I spent with high-maintenance terriers who so easily broke my heart.

I was at the vet with Sadie for a checkup. Becca had died earlier that year. I took all my dogs to the vet at the same time, even if the appointment was only for one of the dogs, then we'd all head off to the Poudre River right down the street. I had brought her in from the car to the vet's air-conditioned office and she patiently laid down by my chair while I waited for Sadie's checkup. The vet had been with me through a few dogs and she was aware of my blindness when it came to noticing my dogs end-of-life issues.

"So, Jesse doesn't look so great. When did she start not being able to get up on her own?"

What? She gets up fine, I thought.

"Come on, Jesse, let's get up, show her."

Jesse didn't move, and it dawned on me that I was supposed to let her go, right there. Right then. I called my son who was romancing his high school sweetheart sailing on Lake

Sherwood on a used Sunfish I had bought him earlier that year. It was old but functional and, apparently, very romantic. He had his phone.

"Dan, the vet thinks Jesse should go. She's in pain and can't get up. Do you want to come to say goodbye?"

"Um, no, that's okay. I trust you." Far cry from just a few years ago when he thought that I was ushering Becca to an early and unnecessary death.

I called Sarah who was playing soccer for University of Idaho and had adopted her Toby two years before. She cried but said she trusted me too. I was overwhelmed. My kids trusted me. I didn't know what to say. I told her to tell a friend and have a good cry, but Jesse had lived a marvelous life and I'm sure she loved Sarah a whole lot. I hung up.

I let Jesse go. When I got back her paw print embedded in clay, and the requisite flowered box with her ashes, I was surprised at its heft. The label on top said "Jesse Roberts, August 3, 2003. Weight 100 lbs." Damn.

* * *

It was Sadie and me now. And Dan, of course. He used to pick her up, hold her close to his face, and in a little squeaky voice say, "We love each other and we're going to get married." It was the funniest thing. Naturally, I told all his girlfriends and I'd even imitate him on family holidays for entertainment. I still do. And he did it again, on Sadie's last Christmas in front of everybody. By then, Sadie was a little blind, and a little deaf, but much less resistant.

When Dan was in high school, he and a friend made a movie about the death of a dog and it may have involved Dan's BB gun. All I remember is the part where Dan's friend ran up to the house, my dog Sadie limp in his arms and sobbing, "She's dead, she's dead," and Sadie blinking open one eye as if to reassure me she was only acting. I knew then she loved me even though at times, I wasn't sure.

I called her 'Sadie O'Grady, She's My Lady' and I'd sing to her in hopes she'd mellow out and one day accept my offers to snuggle. Sadie didn't snuggle. I've learned in the last few years dogs don't really like to be enveloped in a constricting hug and the good dogs will tense and put up with it; the less disciplined dogs will growl, flatten their ears back and sometimes nip their surprised humans who just wanted to show love and affection to the dog. Sadie curled her lips at times, and we'd laugh at her but judiciously let her go. She'd sleep with me at night at one end of the bed, rarely close enough to spoon but it was good enough.

She was a warrior, forever seeking an enemy who deserved her attention. If it wasn't the squirrels twenty feet up a cottonwood, it was the neon green snakes in the backyard. If Jake hadn't of killed all the koi in the pond, she would've jumped in gladly to participate in the mass murder though her snake-killing skills were more precise and tidier than Jake's.

She was also more discriminating than Jake when being approached by dogs on the bike path. Jake showed his teeth to all dogs, his tongue darting in and out between low-throttled growls, as if anticipating the taste of the offending dog's blood. Sadie only hated small terriers, not unlike herself. She'd bark at big dogs but would happily run with them if I let her off leash. Sadie was the only dog I trusted completely. Her judgment was unassailable.

CHAPTER 10

DYLAN

2004-2006

I am incapable of saying no to my kids when they ask for another dog. There's always a reason and I usually don't delve too much into why. I'm also aware I will be caring for these dogs long after the kids leave. Although, I give kudos to Sarah for not leaving Toby with me for longer than was necessary—he was hers and she took responsibility.

Dan wanted his own dog again. This time, no more crazy terriers. He wanted a big lovable boy he could wrestle and hike mountains and attract girls with. We hadn't spent long on Petfinder.com when we found 'Sampson,' a large yellow lab

Husky mix with a big tongue curling up over his muzzle and up his nose, as if he had a piece of peanut butter stuck up there and was trying to lick it off.

I'm not sure why the online photo did it for me, but I called Underground Rescue in nearby Greeley and scheduled a visit. The description said he was about three years old, maybe fifty-five pounds, friendly and smart. Some of that was true—he was very friendly and very smart.

We drove there after Dan's baseball practice. It was already dark. I rang the doorbell, but they wouldn't let us in. A waft of cigarette smoke poured out with an older lady accompanied by a massive dog on a leash.

"Did you bring a leash and your check?" she croaked. Well, yes, but we were here to meet him. She took her leash off him, I put mine on and gave her the check. She wished us good luck, shutting the door behind her.

He smelled awful. And he was not three years old and fifty-five pounds. Dan and I looked at each other puzzled. How could this long-limbed, big-chested dog with muscled haunches and a deliberate slow-moving manner be only "three or so" and not at least seventy-five pounds? We walked him around the block, both of us trying to decide if we were going to take this plodding, stinky dog home.

"We have to change his name," Dan spoke first. We put him in the car and went back to Fort Collins. A friend of mine and I still joke about how old and big this dog really was. We figured seven or eight years old and maybe ninety pounds

'Sampson' became Dylan after the singer/songwriter, and he was the best dog. I say that with apologies to Sadie since I still consider her my most well-loved dog, but she didn't have the gene that made dogs want to please their humans. She had the opposite gene, like a cat—she ruled her kingdom with diffidence and only begrudgingly showed affection. Just a little ding against her but it's what made her special. She was a 'cat-dog.'

Becca, Jesse, and Jake had all died, and Sadie was my lone dog at the time. Sarah had taken Toby back to school with her a year ago but would leave Toby with us during her last semester in college while she lived in Spain. Dan had eighteen months left of high school and he would be leaving for college without Dylan. I'd have a little girl dog and a big boy dog, and it felt perfect.

Despite Sadie's natural tendency to treat new dogs in the household with disdain, she also had a realistic side that won the tug of war. She could either pout in the corner or start a new tribe with the big yellow guy trying to get her attention. The pendulum was swinging back to larger dogs. She knew she had to throw her weight around and the best way to do that was to get Dylan on her side

Dylan loved the frisbee and tennis balls, though his return rate was never much over fifty percent. He'd lose interest if Dan, with his powerful pitching arm, threw it too far. Dylan would sit, yawn, then turn back towards home. Sadie wouldn't fetch a ball if you paid her in chicken nuggets, but she snickered at Dylan's half-assed attempt to honor his lab lineage. Eventually, I'd catch her playing with Dylan's massive tail then running with him out by the lake near our house. I even caught her sleeping with him on the couch, tucked up against the back of his neck.

Dylan didn't need a leash. He could have been a model dog at an obedience/training school, the school's instructors using him to show prospective clients how a good dog behaves.

But he was smart, too, not just a dog who learned some tricks. If he had had opposable thumbs, he could've made dinner.

He loved to run. Our jaunts on the bike path and foothills trails reminded me of Becca as the miles passed, in sync, content with the landscape, the movement and the company. I talked to him on the slower runs, asking him if he was having a good time. I'd veer into my thoughts about the other dogs or tell him about my day. Sometimes, we'd stop by the Poudre River so he could cool down and we'd sit by the river's bank for a few minutes, watching ducks and debris flow downstream. I felt lucky to be with this dog and hoped that his generous nature and confidence would instill similar qualities in me.

Car rides were a joy for him, his big head in my rear-view mirror poking out the window, spewing saliva down the side of the old Subaru. Sadie liked the front seat but soon took to the back, standing on the arm rest of the opposite window from Dylan, her snout inching out the window. I'd tease and say that she was copying Dylan, but she ignored me.

I wondered what the people behind me thought, looking at this massive yellow head ducking in and out of a window and a tiny nose doing the same thing on the other side. Sometimes I'd yell at them to get their heads in, threatening to roll up the window the whole way. Once I nearly killed them both, rolling up the electric windows before they had time to withdraw their heads into the body of the car. I still feel queasy about it.

A few months after Dylan came to live with us, I was headed out to an event at the local roller rink. It was a fundraiser for a cause I supported and thought maybe I should strap on the skates again and hopefully not hurt myself. Dan was home alone, and I told him to make sure Dylan was okay. The skies were murky with a storm forming. Dylan was afraid of thunder and I told Dan to be mindful. When I got home, the door was wide open, it had rained and thundered, and the wind had forced the door open. Dan hadn't noticed which made me think his girlfriend had been visiting.

"Where's Dylan, for Christ's sake, where's Dylan?"

I screamed at Dan. Sadie was curled up on the couch and had not taken the opportunity to wander outside during the storm, flashbacks to the last time she did that and ended up at Larimer Humane Society for a weekend. Dan knew he screwed up and we jumped on our bikes and took different directions on the bike path, calling out Dylan's name. It was ten o'clock at night. He was nowhere to be found. I was sure he was looking for me, in a panic, unable to find his way home.

This is when I became the dog and attempted to feel his terror. Or maybe what decisions he's made. It felt to me like he was running the bike path again, hoping I was out there. Unable to find him, I went to bed bereft and convinced he had been hit by a car.

I was at Larimer Humane Society when it opened the next day. I didn't trust them to tell me over the phone that no yellow lab/Husky mix had shown up during the night. I wanted to see for myself. The woman at the counter stopped me halfway through my panicked narrative and said that someone had just called asking if anyone was looking for a big yellow lab. She gave me the woman's number and I went and sat in my car, nearly hysterical with relief as I described Dylan perfectly.

"Where are you? I'll come get him!" The woman hesitated on the other end of the phone, and I thought, why isn't she telling me? Is she keeping him? I'll find her and punch her in the throat. But wait, why would she call Larimer Humane and leave her number?

"Well, I just wanted to make sure you weren't the person who dropped him off during that rainstorm at Edora Park and left him terrified and hiding underneath one of those huge spruce trees. And maybe you've changed your mind and want him back."

"What? What? Someone left him? What are you talking about?"

I was horrified but it did occur to me that maybe they saw him crossing Drake Road, a major street near us and didn't want him to get hit. I couldn't imagine anyone not wanting him, but it was possible that they couldn't take him home. But why dump him in a rain and thunderstorm, shaking and terrified?

The woman described how she had been caught in the storm on her bike and was sitting under one of the shelter areas in the park to ride out the worst of the storm when she saw a car drive up and kick Dylan out the door. She got him to come to her and they stayed together like that for a while. When the rain stopped, she walked him and her bike to her apartment. He spent the night. He had his license on his collar plus his name with my phone number.

She didn't call me first because she wanted to make sure that I wasn't the awful person who did this. It all made sense, of course, and she even asked me if I wanted to give him up. I told her he was the smartest and best dog in the world except for a little issue with thunder. I also blamed my son and his teenage hormones, and she laughed then told me where to meet her. Dylan was never left home alone again.

It wasn't just thunder that rankled Dylan. He harbored a disdain for most men, although he loved my son. But if a guy came to my door who inadvertently sent the wrong signals, Dylan would issue a warning growl.

One time I had a client come to my house and as he stepped in, I told him to be respectful and just say hi to Dylan but don't make a fuss.

"But dogs love me!" as he proceeded to get down to Dylan's level, meeting him eye to eye. Then the client abruptly got up and walked toward me. Dylan bit through his jeans on his calf, leaving a red mark that turned into a growing bruise by the time he left. While the guy was doing everything you shouldn't do, I was telling him to get up and ignore Dylan. Instead, he sent Dylan a clear signal that he was challenging him and there was nothing he could do about it. Dylan begged to differ. I hoped my homeowner's insurance covered vigilante dogs.

Dylan made me feel safe. His presence meant I didn't always have to be the one protecting everyone else, standing between my dogs and any random evil that could infiltrate our tribe. Neither did I have to worry that he was going to, without provocation, attack strangers who harbored no bad intentions. I had no problem with the incident with my client—I should have been more proactive and stepped in earlier. I learned my lesson, and now I insist people behave around my dogs and not be so arrogant as to think they know what they're doing. My dogs aren't to be trifled with. No dog should be trifled with.

It felt good to have such a handsome burly guy protect me and my family, inserting his athletic four-legged self between us and all those who would do us harm. People turned and looked as we ran along the bike path or sauntered through the crowds in Fort Collins's Old Town district, Dylan alert and confident, staying close to my side, undisturbed by the silly antics of the rest of the world. I was so proud of him. Dylan loved to run the fields by my friend's farmhouse. We'd go over on a late afternoon, and I'd let him run free because he was the only dog I ever had that would come when called. Even Sadie had to stay behind the fence, too prone to chase a rabbit down a real rabbit hole and not return. Dylan ignored the horses and set out to just run. It made me so happy to see him so happy.

I thought back to when we first adopted Dylan and the odd behavior of his foster mom, the older lady with the smoking habit. I wanted to ask her how anyone could give up this dog. She was a foster volunteer for Underground Rescue, and they didn't share much with me when I first called them about Sampson aka Dylan.

"He's a stray," they said, "found wandering down by the railroad downtown."

How could that happen? Dylan was the definition of a gentleman dog—kind, attentive, protective, and affectionate. If I had been his foster mom, I would have been a 'foster failure,' someone who fosters dogs then ends up adopting them. Most likely, the foster mom was in over her head with too many foster dogs and she may have been teetering on that fine line between 'fun household' and 'dog hoarding.' There were just too many different yips and yaps and barks when we rang the doorbell the night we adopted Dylan.

Two years passed since Dylan joined our family. By then, I had reluctantly taken in Zach, a freaked-out rat terrier newly recovered from heartworm. A vet student had rescued him from death's door and took on the onerous process of curing him of the illness. She begged me to take him because I already had a terrier and I knew their ways.

No, I didn't. I barely understood Sadie and she often stunned me with an unexpected act of kindness or cruelty. I gave in. I was more than 'teetering' on that fine line. It felt like I had taken a face plant.

Sarah graduated college and moved to a friend's condo with her dog Toby but came back for a bit when it didn't work out. Four dogs were overwhelming for me. I liked a semi-clean house and the knowledge that things would be where I left them. That slowly eroded over the next few months, stressing me out more than I realized.

And I met a man. His name was John, and he had a dog—a beautiful Bernese named Lily. He and I would meet by the old quarries located about equal distances from each of our homes and run with our dogs, Dylan loping beside me and Sadie and Zach investigating any possible snake holes, looking up occasionally to make sure we hadn't disappeared. It had been a few years since I bothered dating and it was a frightening ordeal at first, but we fell into a rhythm of running the dogs in the late afternoon, dinner at his house and maybe I'd stay over, but it wasn't often.

I wanted our dogs to bring us closer, something we had in common other than our Boston childhood and liberal (somewhat) politics, but I don't think he liked my dogs. By this time, I was in my fifties and believed I had made too many errors in judgment to trust myself again. Do I trust my decision to date

John and not question the nagging feelings I got about his attitude with my dogs? Change is supposed to be uncomfortable, I argued with myself, but I was relieved and happy to get home and fall into bed with my three dogs. They were happy, too.

Sarah was usually at home with Toby and cared for my dogs while I was out, but I knew they'd be waiting for me to come back, sitting by the door at midnight, wondering where I was. If I brought them to John's, they weren't allowed in his room. It was the beginning of the end. I should have known then, but I was never great at reading the writing on the wall. It dragged on for too long. It was the night he stayed over at my house and wouldn't allow the dogs in my room.

"They're crybabies. You spoil them."

Them were, or should've been, fightin' words. But I still didn't break it off.

Instead, I lay in tears, questioning every decision I had ever made. I wanted to spend the night on the living room couch with my dogs, Zach and Sadie laying asleep on my chest and legs, and Dylan on his dog bed close enough for me to touch his head. I knew it would mean I probably wouldn't date again.

One afternoon, John and I were running the dogs in the quarry and Dylan was having a difficult time peeing and pooing. Watching him was painful. I turned around, gathered up my dogs and headed home. I told John I'd keep him posted. The vet didn't have the portable x-ray at the office that morning but would get the vet radiologist over that afternoon with her portable machine. It didn't take long to diagnose Dylan: prostate cancer. It was now in his spine. It was a slow-growing cancer and I immediately judged his previous owners.

Was this why his owners dumped him, not able to afford treatment? How did I not know? In hindsight, Dylan had a problem with his penis, standing erect at inappropriate moments and for too long, forcing him to wobble uncomfortably. I had mentioned it to my vet, but she shrugged her shoulders and said that some dogs were just like that. What would I have done anyway? Spend thousands on chemo or radiation? It might have been a lot less when it was first diagnosed but I didn't have that luxury anymore. I had only been his human for two years and, damn it, not much longer.

I took him back out to the farm, so he could run, but this time it was a slow lope. I cooked a steak and sweet potatoes for him then walked him near the Poudre River. We had a long talk about how I felt about him, how much I loved him. How proud I was of him, and how Sadie would miss him terribly. I thanked him for being so nice to Zach when he needed a sane male role model.

Dan was a freshman at college and on the bus going to a baseball game where he would pitch. I probably should have waited until the game was over before calling, but I needed to talk to someone. I usually talked to Dylan when I was upset. Dan was distressed and swore he would never get another dog. I understood. Sometimes I say the same thing.

It didn't take long at the vet's. I'm always surprised by euthanasia and how quickly a dog succumbs to the drugs, big or little. I lay on the blanket next to Dylan as he died, telling him again and again what a good boy he was, and how he was the best dog ever, and how lucky I was to have him in my life. I whispered to him that if he finds out that dogs reincarnate, could he try and make sure he comes back to see me? Maybe choose me again?

I'm still waiting.

John and I dated for another couple of months and even went on a sailing trip together. Later, John would confess that he jumped the gun, asking me to go on the two-week trip. Even before we left, he thought I was too loud and opinionated. He also thought I had a problem with crazy dogs. I knew I shouldn't have gone, but I was trying to be a different person than who I was. I wanted to be daring and spontaneous, saying yes when I wanted to say a firm "No!"

John dumped me on that trip. It was humiliating, and I couldn't enjoy what I would normally consider heaven—a fifty-foot sloop, gorgeous May days in the Caribbean, an emerald ocean, white sand beaches, and a multitude of delicacies straight from the ocean.

And I missed my dogs.

CHAPTER 11

ZACH

2005–2016

The first time I saw Zach, he was running with five Australian Shepherds around the ponds where I was walking with Sadie and Dylan. He shot past his buddies like a black and white bullet. His human, Susan, had found him on death row in Kentucky where she was visiting her mom and helping her choose a dog from the local shelter. A high-kill shelter.

"He's got heartworm and he's a stray. Too much effort to save him. We don't have the resources." Zach was one day from euthanasia. Susan fell in love with the five-pound Zach and negotiated the medicine he needed, telling them she was a vet student at Colorado State University in Fort Collins, CO and she knew what to do with it.

Weeks later, he was allowed physical exercise and that's when he nearly ran into Sadie who bared her teeth at him, not knowing he was on his maiden flight as a healthy, albeit under-weight, dog alive and really kicking. He ran one way, then the other, then took huge leaps around rocks, other dogs, and large puddles. Frenetic, ecstatic—he was happy to be alive and hangin' with his friends.

Zach was a rat terrier. Memories of Jake haunted me. These dogs were popular on Kentucky horse ranches, killing rats in the barns and chasing the other dogs for the hell of it. Zach didn't do any of these things as far as I could see but, despite Susan's enthusiasm about his ability to fit in with my little tribe, I did not want this lunatic.

Sadie thought him a fool. I knew Susan from her neighbor, a client of mine, and she had asked if I wanted another dog. Her dad had forbidden any addition to her clan. Now that Zach was healthy, he had to go.

"You'll love this dog, you already have a terrier, so you know."

I didn't know. Why did she keep saying that? Sadie did listen to me, if reluctantly, and was a confident dog, having had bigger dogs as role models. She rarely behaved badly and possessed an innate sense of who did or didn't appreciate her and acted accordingly. In that sense, I thought of her as a badass who had nothing to prove. If that were a terrier temperament, I'd take him on, but he acted crazy and then fearful and submissive. He was a nutcase.

I said no, but I'd think about it. She called me five times. I agreed to meet him one-on-one at her house without all my dogs or hers. He was shaking and so skinny, I could see ribs poking out the side.

"He'll gain some weight eventually," Susan smiled, hoping I would scoop him up and rush him home for a more formal meet 'n greet with my dogs. I still wasn't sure. Within a week, he had joined us, but only because Susan was persistent, not because I had fully committed. A few days later, my cleaning lady arrived with her seven-year-old son who was not feeling well.

"I had nowhere to bring him."

I suggested that she go home and not worry about my house. No, I need the money, she apologized. I offered to pay her, but she smiled no.

I put Zach in my bedroom, closed the door tight and told her she didn't need to clean there today. She and I both spoke carefully to her son, admonishing him to not go in my bedroom since I had a new dog and didn't know what he would do. I went out to my office in the back of the house and five minutes later, there was a loud kid scream and I went running. His mother got there first.

Her son had entered my room, crawled under the bed where Zach lay trembling and tried to pull him out. Zach got him good. But I didn't blame the dog. The kid didn't listen, lesson learned. I paid for the Urgent Care visit. He had a nasty bruise on his face and the mother told the doctor she knew the dog didn't have rabies, but she wouldn't tell him who owned him. I was grateful. Unfortunately, dogs are always paying for our mistakes.

A couple months later, Dan arrived home from college for a short visit. Neither Sarah nor I had told Dan that I had got another dog. Before he had left, he wanted me to promise that I wouldn't get any more dogs. I refused, of course. It wasn't his call. We still had Dylan, Sarah's Toby, and Sadie. We hid Zach in my office until Dan had greeted all the other dogs. Then I let Zach out and he went tearing out to the living room, wagging his nub of a tail furiously.

"What the hell is this?" I knew Dan was reliving the crazy-ass Jake days and I assured him that Zach wasn't like that, at least not exactly.

"He did bite a kid last week, but it wasn't his fault." It was a weak defense. I told Dan Zach didn't tolerate teasing, close encounters face-to-face, or quick movements. The Jake comparison *was* uncanny. Back then, we had had notes on our front door that warned visitors to not look Jake directly in the eyes. I wondered if we might have to do that again.

I warned when I headed out to work, "Don't screw with him, Dan." The story goes that Dan wanted to blow raspberries on Zach's belly. Zach clamped down hard on Dan's nose which left him bleeding and wondering if he should go to ER. No doubt Sarah laughed at him. They decided he wasn't dying, and Dan thought he could get away with me not noticing for at least a day or two. They didn't want me to say, "I told you so." I wouldn't have. I would have screamed it at the top of my lungs. It was rare when I was conceded a win with those two.

From then on, they went about discovering Zach's quirks. For the rest of Zach's life, when my kids stopped by with friends, they'd say, "Watch this!," slap the leather couch hard and Zach would jump on the couch and curl his lips. His low terrier growl would get more intense and just before he'd pounce, everyone would stop and run like hell, laughing at him. I'd run over and hold him like a baby, soothing him while he looked in their direction, his lips still curled.

I was hooked. Besides being gorgeous, Zach loved me dearly. He was never far and slept under the covers with me until almost the very end, a couple weeks before he died. And then it was only because he couldn't get up to climb the three doggie stairs to my bed. And I was afraid to sleep with him because he was in so much pain. But in the intervening eleven years, and despite the ever-present danger of sneak attacks, he was my baby. I had a type—unpredictable, slightly dangerous, and handsome. Though I believe that Jake was diagnosable—borderline, sociopath, take your pick—Zach was just needy and scared.

The best part of having Zach was that Sadie found a friend, a more reasonably sized friend. They slept curled up together like yin and yang. Zach was mostly white with two black spots on his back and Sadie was black with some white and brown. They looked like brother and sister though they were two different breeds. Zach deferred to her when it came to food or seating arrangements in the car and even on the couch. He tried to bite her a couple of times when they were older, and he was hurting. I didn't know at the time that he, too, like Sadie, was suffering from degenerative disc disease. I just thought he had a momentary lapse in judgment.

When I first got Zach, he would hide out on the far corners of the yard, digging a hole and settling in. He wouldn't answer me when I called. During the first heavy snow, I thought he was inside, but realized after a couple of hours that he was nowhere in the house. Donning boots, down coat, gloves, hat, and a flashlight, I went outside. It took a few attempts, kicking over leaf piles covered in snow, but I finally found him, shivering in a small hole he had dug in the southwest corner of the yard, huddled between upturned clay pots.

Why did he do this? Was he afraid of Dylan? Toby had moved out and the other possibility was me or Sadie. I think it was just what he knew. He had been a stray and I'm sure he found the least vulnerable spots to rest when he was alone out there. It broke my heart. The doggie door remained closed during nasty weather after that.

Zach also ran, not as in joyful running the fields and racing your fellow canines—but in escaping the backyard or running out the front door and down the street as if he were once again a street dog and had to fend for himself. Many times, I'd get the call saying, "We have your dog, Zach." His name and my number were written large on his tag. Sometimes I got the call where they say that they could read the number to call me, but he wouldn't come to them and he's standing in the middle of the road, dodging traffic. He never went far. If I couldn't be there in three minutes, I'd tell the person on the phone to sit quietly, call his name but don't grab him, I'd say, just wait, I'll be right there. Or I'd suggest they open their car door so he could jump in. It always worked and I'm grateful to all my neighbors.

One time he jumped out the car window while I was driving slowly through a neighborhood, looking for a house number. He had spotted another rat terrier and out the window he went. I panicked, called Animal Control, a friend to come help. I begged St. Francis to guide me through the rural streets in the right direction. We were also only about a half mile from the ponds and maybe he sensed that. After a frantic thirty minutes, driving up and down the alleys and dirt streets, calling his name, I pulled over and got out, yelling his name one final time before giving up. His head peeked out from a backyard. I opened the passenger door and he casually jumped in.

"You're such an ass, Zach," I said reaching over to kiss him. My anxiety over the possibility of losing him shook me. As much as I hadn't wanted another dog, I had another dog. And he needed me. As a skilled worrier, I imagined him getting hit by a car, or attacked by a big dog, or lost in the wilds of north Fort Collins, ducking in and out of yards, too terrified to trust anyone but me. That never happened, but it could've.

Zach was athletic but timid. Sadie wasn't as agile or strong, but she would try anything, so I signed them up for an agility class. Sadie ran the course quickly, focused, and competitive. When I finally got Zach out there, he would slowly move through the paces, looking at me after each move, either begging to be released from this torture or asking for praise, I could never be sure. He was confident only when Sadie was the only other dog at the facility. He followed her faithfully. There was one time he ran through the course, flying high, scooting through the tunnel, bursting out of it to the next obstacle wide-eyed and frenetic, but he had hit the course, gracefully and in incredible time, according to the trainer.

"Damn, he's a natural and so fast!" She was impressed. But I knew it wouldn't happen ever again. By then, I understood him. He was telling me that he could do it and with great success, but it wasn't his thing. And he never did do it again, just like the time he swam out to meet me in the pond, got hit on the head with a stick, and never swam again.

We tried Flyball. A dog navigates several hurdles before grabbing a ball stuck to a wall with Velcro then runs back over the same hurdles.

Sadie picked up the game with intelligence and fierceness, though the hurdles were still too high for her. It was held in a horse arena, and Zach kept looking around for whatever monster inhabited this space. He was terrified. I had to hold him the whole time I took Sadie through her paces. We went back once and the trainer tried to help, but Zach refused. I was glad to be done with that, anyway. We smelled like horseshit and the place was freezing.

CHAPTER 12
SUNNY

2007–2017

I had Sunny for ten years.

I tried to get rid of him shortly after I brought him home. He was trouble and what ailed him was costing me. Adopting Sunny was a colossal mistake, instigated by a brief email asking for people to foster the dogs from the 2007 Malibu wildfire. These dogs had endured a terrifying bus ride over the Rocky Mountains in the middle of winter. A local Colorado rescue had volunteered to drive to California in a large school bus to pick up dogs from an overcrowded shelter in Malibu and bring the dogs back to Loveland, Colorado. Not unusual for a state that consistently brings in more than thirty thousand dogs a year to be placed for adoption.

I sat at my desk while Zach and Sadie lay sleeping in the same dog bed at my feet. A few months before, I had decided to get my master's degree in communications at fifty-six years old. A mid-life crisis, a yearning to fulfill a childhood dream, a final cry into the wilderness to do something important or relevant or good—who knows? But I knew I wanted to write a memoir. I started classes when the housing market was slowing before it finally ground to a halt for the next few years. Not a good thing for a real estate agent paying tuition while not making any money.

I was working on one of my first classroom assignments— write an insightful essay about literary criticism, a topic I had no business attempting. My bachelor's degree was in Technical Journalism, a degree I earned in 1974. When the email about the rescue pups from California arrived in my Inbox, I was writing an excruciatingly bad piece on the Shambhala Buddhist Teachings influence on Ann Waldman's poetry. Sadie and Zach were peacefully sleeping as a snowstorm raged outside. A few days later, I was wishing I had immediately deleted that email. I shut off the computer, stood up, and reached for my coat and boots.

"Off to save another doggie, my sweets! Be kind to whoever I bring home! Protect the homestead and don't pee till I get back and let you out," I shouted Don-Quixote-like, tilting at puppy mills. Honestly, I probably didn't say anything. I got in the car and drove down a slippery, snow-covered College Avenue and headed to Loveland.

The dogs were temporarily housed in crates in a large warehouse with space heaters placed in every other aisle. I imagined the dogs were hoping someone would explain to them why they had left temperate California for a subzero winter in Colorado.

Many of the dogs were taken by the time I got there. Rows of crates were spread across the cement floors. It was freezing. I walked to the back of the building and saw that most of the crates were empty. The dogs that were still there were sleeping or were way too big for me. I was getting older and didn't want to wrangle with a sixty-pound dog lunging at other dogs on the trail. I assumed I would continue being a lousy dog trainer.

Good, I thought, nothing here for me. I don't need another damaged dog. The front door and my calm two-dog life was only yards away when I spotted a chunky smallish dog, squished up against a corner of his crate. No harm in looking at him, I lied to myself.

He was a dull yellow, too round for his height, sitting with his back to me, occasionally looking over his shoulder to see what I was doing. The tag on the crate said his name was Sunny. Aspirational, I assumed.

Trying hard not to construct a story around this pathetic fat boy who couldn't even manage to wag his tail, I turned around and headed to the back of the building to make sure I didn't miss a magnificent and trained Dylan clone, only smaller. I missed the big guy and had searched for another dog like him ever since he died.

I glanced back at the pitiful creature across the warehouse. He was staring at me. Weirdo. I ambled back to that part of the warehouse, watching his eyes follow me as if I were a predator or maybe prey. He didn't seem brave or angry enough to want to take a bite out of me. He was sad, incredibly sad, and looked like he had never had a friend in the world. Damn it. This is where I think I can change a dog's life; reassure them they're loved and wanted. Sometimes I wished I could solve my childhood trauma through a few angst-laden therapy sessions and I would no longer need to save these dogs, who I'm confident could find other families. Why me, for God's sakes? Where was a best friend telling me to put down my checkbook, say goodbye to whatever dog I had picked out, and go home and play with the dogs I already have?

They're not here because I didn't tell anyone what I was doing, knowing they'd try to talk me out of it. Didn't even tell my daughter who would've yelled at me. Not that I didn't need it. Though if Sadie could answer a phone and talk, I would've called *her* for advice.

A family with a young boy came up to Sunny's crate and took him out on a leash while one of the gals who worked there said they were going to do a 'meet 'n greet' first. I would be next. The snow had stopped by then, but the temperature hovered around ten degrees. Sunny pulled back as they opened the door for him. I imagine he felt he was going to die. I wanted to shout for them to put a coat on him or something. He's from Malibu, for Christ's sake!

Two minutes later, they were back, unleashing Sunny and gently guiding him into his metal home. The father fumbled with the latch until he heard it click shut.

"We'll find the right dog," he said to his son, placing his hand on the kid's shoulder as if he was the one who needed comforting. I watched them walk away and leave the warehouse.

"I'll take him." I heard myself saying, as I neared Sunny's crate. He seemed cold and needy and scared. If I had a type, this was it.

His papers said, "Chihuahua Mix." It looked like someone in his lineage was a yellow lab who had an affair with a Chihuahua terrier mutt. He had the shedding double coat of a lab but everything else was neurotic Chihuahua. Weighing twenty-five pounds, he needed to lose a minimum of five pounds, twenty percent of his body mass. One pointy ear stayed up and the other tried hard but with little success. I would later call him a 'trash dog,' because he was obsessed with food as if he had lived near a landfill and fought the local denizens, i.e., rats and seagulls, for the available food. Or his human just overfed him and never exercised him. Or he was just another crazy dog.

From the beginning, Zach hated Sunny. Sunny's first impulse was to run scared from Zach, his tail tucked between his legs, hoping Zach wouldn't catch it and bite it off. Later, once he gained an iota of confidence, Sunny would learn to chase Zach back despite the risk.

A couple of months after Sunny had settled in, he fell asleep in the middle of my crossed legs while I sat on the couch watching TV. His entire body curled into my lap with his nose tucked into the crook of my knee. It was sweet, and I didn't dare move even when my right knee began its familiar ache. Zach walked over and stared at us.

"No, Zach," I whispered, wagging my finger back and forth at him as if he understood what he was about to do was a no-no.

I wasn't going to let him intimidate Sunny while he was in my care. But Sunny sensed the dark presence and quickly woke and scrambled to get down from my lap. Sometimes I just wanted to put Zach in time-out and take away his privileges. At least I wouldn't let him on my lap. I got up and went into the kitchen leaving Zach to reconsider his actions.

Within a month, Sunny was chasing Zach around the yard barking in a monotonous, persistent beat. Zach would put up with it for a couple of turns around the yard then he'd turn and charge Sunny with a viciousness that had all of us running in the other direction. Sadie watched in amusement, occasionally joining in the chase but giving up when it looked like Zach was going to kill Sunny.

Within months, chaos became the new norm at the house. All because I couldn't figure out the Shambhala Dharma influences on Anne Waldman's poetry. A friend had even warned me adding Sunny to the mix was a bad idea, that I should get rid of him as soon as possible. I trusted her judgment, but it was too late—like telling me to not buy a house when I'm sitting at the closing table and had signed the warranty deed or realizing the "I Do" I just said ten minutes ago was a mistake. Things could be undone, but it would take a long time and sometimes accepting the consequences seemed easier.

Sunny's vet pointed out the rotten tooth needing immediate extraction. Typical. All my terriers had bad teeth. But it was his assessment of Sunny's infected anal glands that pushed me to my breaking point. In the beginning, the vet treated Sunny with a series of antibiotics and squeezing his anal glands twice a week, a procedure which irritated them. The meds didn't work and now the vet wanted to remove Sunny's glands with the possible side effect of fecal incontinence. Sunny had been living with us only a few months and he'd already become The Problem Child.

I tried raising the funds to get all this work done, approximately five thousand dollars. I called it The Campaign to Save Sunny's Butt. Clever, but ultimately, a bust. Nobody contributed. He needed to be 're-homed' as they say in the rescue business. It meant the humans had given up. And I had. I felt terrible, especially knowing Sunny was an owner-surrender—his previous human had dumped him at the shelter for unknown reasons. I had also discovered Sunny had gone home with another family for a few days but had returned him just before I showed up at the warehouse. No reason stated.

I circulated a poster with cute photos and an honest description of Sunny's issues, adding he was devoted and cuddly. People don't want to hear the words 'fecal incontinence' when choosing a new dog. I talked to a man on the phone interested in Sunny and he came to meet him at my house. As soon as he walked in the door with his wife, I knew I didn't like him. He was vaguely familiar, possibly someone I had shown houses to long ago. Arrogant and knowing just enough about dogs to risk being bit from Sunny, he turned the poor dog over on his back to show dominance.

I flipped out as did Sunny. Struggling to get up, his eyes imploring me to do something, I grabbed the guys arm and told him to stop. Sunny got his bearings and tried to bite him at the same time.

"This one won't ever amount to anything. Good luck with him," the man got up and sneered at us. It was before I started using the 'F' word as my go to response to everything, so I just slammed the door after him.

"Well, I guess you're here to stay, and I offer my sincere apologies for being an ass. We're even now," I emphasized.

I nodded at Sunny, and he followed me back into the kitchen, knowing there would be a treat. I suspected Zach was disappointed Sunny was still here. I had told him to be nice to Sunny before the guy came, knowing Sunny might leave us. I gave everyone a treat, but I could tell Zach was pissed. He took his little bone-shaped peanut butter biscuit outside, stepping through the doggie door into a freezing rain. If he could have slammed the doggie door's plastic flap, he would've.

I called my former vet who had moved to another town and made an appointment. She recommended an expensive supplement which I gave to Sunny for a month. Repeat if he had problems again. One month later, his anal gland issues subsided, and I only had to repeat the treatment one more time. And that infected tooth? I kept up frequent dental cleanings until I finally had to have it pulled five years later.

* * *

Over the years, I'd find Zach hiding in a corner of the yard many times. Sometimes months would go by and I'd think he finally was done with it, until I'd spend a half hour looking for him, driving the car around neighborhood before I remembered that he'd probably never be done with it. I'd come home and there he was, curled up in a different corner of the yard, for no discernible reason. Other times, he'd duck into the unheated storage room and sit on the concrete floor shivering until I opened it up. It didn't matter that I had been calling for him for an hour. He didn't answer back. I'd open the door and there he was freezing, his tail tucked, maybe a little mad at me, but never mad enough that he didn't enjoy the hugs and treats I gave him while asking for his forgiveness. "Why didn't you bark, you little shit?" I'd question him in a high sing-songy way, careful not to show that *I* was mad.

Every time he'd disappear, the various ways he could suffer and die would cross my mind in snapshots of tragedy. Did he escape and get run over? Did he eat something poisonous while I was out looking for him and he was writhing in abdominal distress? Did he go ballistic and attack Sunny who finally snapped and—after being bullied by Zach for years—fought back and won? Was his brain being destroyed by leftover heartworms not killed by his treatment, and he succumbed to the equivalent of mad cow disease?

Unreasonable fears for most people and worthy of a trip or two to the therapist, but I never was able to not worry about him—was he happy, did he really hate Sunny, why was he so hostile to other dogs (except for Sadie, who he adored), was he in pain, what was populating his nightmares? The only thing I could do was hold him and sing.

I don't remember worrying this much about my kids. They were able to talk and told me when I was needed. When Zach's behavior turned random, lacking any obvious cause, I'd beg him to come tell me what was wrong.

"Just nod your head, okay, Zach? Are you in pain?" I'd sit in front of him, willing him to nod his head or attempt the "ro-ro-

ro-ro" sounds I thought were rat terriers clear attempt at talking.

"Why do you hate Sunny so much?"

"Are worms eating your brain?"

"Are you just a simple asshole?"

The last one was mean, but justified.

Every time I watched Zach tiptoe his way across the room, avoiding whatever demons stalked him, I saw myself, skirting around the corners of my childhood, hoping to not be noticed. I didn't physically cower in fear, yet I preferred protected spaces like the small attic room I hid in, or the wide built-in platform shelf in my bedroom where I read for hours, the misshapen shrub in the backyard that welcomed my body as if it grew like that to harbor me—a troubled and anxious kid seeking sanctuary in an earthy, green-bowed church. Even if my Mom had asked me what was wrong, I couldn't have told her.

By now it was clear to me I rescued emotionally distressed dogs because they reminded me of me. As much as I wanted to be known and loved, it meant being visible and vulnerable. Though, to watch Zach skulk around the room with one shoulder tight against the wall was as painful as it was funny. The only thing I knew to do was to rock him like a baby. Sometimes my kids and I would laugh so hard at his antics that he would stare at us with these strange human button eyes, and I could detect a hint of shame.

"Stop everyone! You're all just a bunch of bullies, you're embarrassing Zach!"

I couldn't help it; it's how I would have felt.

Like all my terriers, Zach had dental problems. They never got better even after losing one tooth after the other. I tried to find a correlation between his bout with heartworm and the required toxic medication and his horrible dentine, but couldn't. His issues were so pervasive that I believe the arsenic in the treatment medication caused him no end of troubles, especially dental disease. Three times a year, he went in for a cleaning and one or two extractions.

"Brush his teeth!" my vet would say. I told him that I couldn't afford the ER trip I would have to take if I ever approached Zach, armed with a small finger-toothbrush covered in chicken-flavored toothpaste, with the intention of cleaning his teeth. I told him I'd do it if he would treat *me* for free.

Zach's biting issues never went away. When Sarah started dating Cody, now her husband, Zach reached up and bit him on the forehead after an attempt to kiss Sarah, who was foolishly holding Zach in her lap. It never occurred to me to blame Zach for any of his behavior. I accepted it and worked hard to predict what would be his next step.

I wasn't always successful. Dan was home for the summer from college, and we had gone to watch his former baseball team play the championship game after a trip to the vet with just Zach. I had a short leather leash for vet trips—it kept the dog in check and told people to stay away from my dog or he'll set free the rage he feels for innocent dogs and their ignorant owners.

Dan's team won and as we stood right by the low chain link fence between the fans and the players, someone threw me a championship hat that skimmed my head and dropped behind me and right between my legs where Zach sat, watchful and possibly paranoid. There was a slight tug of the leash and I looked down to see if Zach needed something when Dan tapped me on the shoulder and said that Zach had just bit this guy on the face.

"What?" I said incredulously. "He's never done that before! What did you do?" Dan, to his credit, kept a straight face, shrugging his shoulders in solidarity. There were two puncture marks on the guys face, rapidly bruising. His wife stood by, trying not to laugh.

"I just reached down to grab the hat and this freak jumped out and bit me." Poor guy, we knew how he felt, but that was my hat and he was stealing it, so.... was I wrong in being proud and a little teary-eyed knowing that Zach had my back?

Dan, Zach, and I left quickly and made sure the guy didn't see us get in the car. I expected a summons for 'vicious dog' in the next few weeks, but it never came. The guy's wife probably told him that he stole the hat and he deserved the four-fanged reprimand.

Sunny wasn't a 'bad' dog—he was just a pain in the ass. Like the kid who pushes Johnny into the girl ahead of him in line and then acts all innocent when the teacher starts yelling at Johnny. Sunny also 'fear-pissed'—anytime he felt anxious, he'd lift his leg on a side chair or the couch or the side of my bed and let a stream go.

In the last ten years with him, I caught him peeing in the house only once. I was out in the yard but had come back in without Sunny hearing me. It was the first indication of his impending hearing loss. I stood transfixed, watching Sunny pee on the wall in the living room. He jumped at my string of invectives and ran outside. Having given up on correcting his behavior long ago, I grabbed a paper towel and vinegar and cleaned it up.

But he loved me. Not that my other dogs didn't love me. Zach's love was a needy, frantic affection, annoying in its persistence, yet with an element of danger if we refused his advances. Sadie was aloof and resistant to snuggles and kisses, refusing to come when called unless it meant a treat or a walk. But when she was younger, I'd find her asleep tight against my back in bed when the nights turned cold. I could pet her then. She'd stretch, and sigh and I knew she was happy. We both were.

Sunny stood naked in his devotion to me. He knew it annoyed me to clean up after his 'accidents,' especially if I stepped in his pee early in the morning. Every so often, there'd be a long thin poop, skirting the edges. He knew I hated him barking after Zach fifty times in a row, the same pitch and tone, the same seconds between each bark as if he was a canine metronome, enraging anyone who hears it. He'd also rear up like a miniature horse, his front feet paddling furiously, his bark intensified, any time there were other dogs on the Poudre Trail, where we ran and walked daily.

We both knew if I dropped his leash, he'd pretend he didn't notice he had his freedom. He didn't really want it. He was a faker, his bravado a veneer concealing a scaredy-cat dog who only wanted food, any food, and the comfort of sleeping next to Sadie. And he wanted my forgiveness, over and over, hoping to convince me he didn't really mean to do anything bad.

And I loved Sunny back. I'm not sure when I began to take comfort in his presence. Picking him up and shouldering him like a sack of potatoes initially frightened him, but with his front legs wrapped around my left shoulder and my right hand cupping his butt, we'd dance around the house, his wide-eyed look of terror eventually relaxing. If I were a betting person, I'd wager a hundred bucks Sunny flaunted his position as 'chosen dog' over Zach who'd slink out the doggie door and pout in a freshly dug hole near the back gate.

When the dogs were younger, our house could be a battle-field, one dog threatening another for food or a place to rest. Sadie always won the food contest. If she neared Zach's or Sunny's food bowl, they'd back away in deference and let her finish their meal. I had to stop it. Sadie was a mere ten pounds but anything over, and she'd start looking like those fat Chihuahuas clutched under the armpits of an older woman with a limp. I wasn't going to be one of them, despite my issues with an old knee injury. Zach tried to steal Sunny's food but as a former garbage dog, Sunny was not intimidated. Zach left him alone after a vicious fight.

It happened one night, a few months after Sunny joined us.

I was always on high alert with him and Zach, both wary of each other to the point they'd circle each other a few times and then go in different directions. One morning I was careless, and served breakfast a little too fast, placing the bowls closer than normal. Sunny inhaled his food and then turned to Zach.

Zach had beautiful brown eyes, perfectly round, otherworldly in their color and shape, as if drawn by Margaret Keane, the artist of the 'Big Eye' paintings. He lowered his head. As the room quieted, I turned back to the dogs and saw Zach's face, his eyes popping out of his head. The attack was swift. Despite his severe dental issues, Zach tore into Sunny. But this was about food and not bed spaces or toys or Sadie or my affection.

Sunny stood his ground, and snarled back, snapping, and licking his mouth. Sadie scooted out through the doggie door, not one to get involved in boys' silly skirmishes. Zach backed away and Sunny tried to finish Zach's food before I grabbed his collar and put him in my bedroom. The entire fight took less than twenty seconds.

They still bickered and growled occasionally but never fought like that again.

Naptime was Zach's chance to exert his dominance once more. Both dogs loved sleeping with Sadie. As did I, of course, but I wasn't granted the privilege very often. If Sunny and Sadie were in one of the ten dog beds strewn throughout the house, Zach would slowly walk over to them and stand over Sunny. Sometimes it took a few minutes before Sunny got up and walked away. I'd watch, hoping to see some subtle exchange of sounds or tics or eye movement that would indicate Zach's need to sleep next to his beloved, and his willingness to hurt Sunny in order to get his way.

Sunny's eyes stared off into the distance, as if his feigned imperception of Zach's threat would make it all go away. It never did. Sunny always lost and I was there to console him, wrapping my arms around his yellow body, telling him Zach was a bully and I would always protect him. I never figured out how they communicated, though it was clear what was said.

As Zach grew more irritated with Sunny, and I grew more protective, lines were drawn, and relationships were changed. I didn't want it to happen, and maybe this what was meant when my friend told me to get rid of Sunny.

Sunny became the 'favored' dog, not because he was well-behaved or even easy-going. He was an ass, according to all connotations of the word. I never wondered why Sunny was 'owner-surrendered.' I even doubted whether he and his owner were a victim of the Malibu wildfires, the owner surrendering him tearfully, unable to care for her cherished puppy, forced to leave him at a shelter with too many residents. Bullshit story. As months and years passed, and his personality emerged, I figured he was a recalcitrant, unapologetic jerk, who ate anything that resembled food and had a personality that pissed off other dogs. His first response when someone attempted to pick him up or hug him, was to freak out and take a half-hearted swipe at the offender. Even I had to be careful when approaching him from behind, until I realized he was deaf.

Once again, I felt sorry for a dog who just needed under-standing, a guiding hand, an observant vet, and the uncondi-tional love of someone, anyone. Sometimes I'm convinced it's arrogance that seeps into our decision-making—'our' meaning those of us who keep rescuing difficult dogs—as if only we had the skills and magic to heal these recalcitrant dogs.

I know my kids thought I had gone insane by then. I may have. In a deeper examination of my motives, I'd have to say it was one of two things—I craved drama, or I was still saving my child self over and over. Now that Sadie and Zach were adjusting well—Zach's fear biting had subsided, and Sadie and I, after six years, had established a subtle rhythm of when I could show affection and when it would be discouraged. I may want drama unconsciously or maybe it was saving myself over and over, but more likely it was because once I've imagined seeing a suffering dog's soul, I can't let it go. He (or she) must come home with me.

People always say, "Oh, you have a big heart" or "you're such a great person," but the truth is people like me have no boundaries. No hard and fast rules designed to protect us from going broke from the veterinarian bills or having our home and yard destroyed or ruining any chance we have of developing our human relationships because our dogs 'need' us to be home. My home is not necessarily the ideal situation for every dog. Sunny would have been happier as the only and most loved dog.

Sunny was no one's favorite dog and he should've been. He deserved it, hell, we all deserve to be someone's favorite.

* * *

Sadie was her happiest when I'd take all the dogs and let them run around the ponds behind Animal House, a local no-kill shelter. It was private property, owned by the gravel company and no one was allowed, but dog people were there every day. Occasionally some horses with their riders would stroll by, rendering all my dogs apoplectic. I'd throw sticks in the water and Sadie would jump in and swim furiously out to get them. She'd bark until I did it again.

It was an unusual for a ten-pound toy fox terrier to love the water and her joy and enthusiasm for swimming shamed my other dogs into getting in the water at least up to their knees. Sometimes my two male terriers would slowly swim out to where she was towing in a stick too big for her. If it happened to hit them in the face, they'd cry and quickly come back to shore. Sadie's opinion of them sunk a bit lower.

It was late morning on a hot August day when we headed

out to the ponds with treats and poop bags. This is the day, I thought. I had worn my bathing suit and would jump in the water with Sadie, fully expecting the boys to finally join us, swimming out to the middle, grinning and laughing, happy to be in a cool, refreshing pond, hangin' with their best buds.

I pulled off my T-shirt and shorts, took off my sneakers and waded in while throwing a stick out in front of me. Sadie sprung off the boulder she was sitting on and headed out. The two boys paced the strip of sand, whining, torn between their reluctance to swim and being left behind. Zach came first, furiously paddling out to where I floated on my back, shouting encouragement. I watched Sunny venture in, but he acted as if he had never been in water before. His dog paddle looked more like a slap, high and hard, spraying water in his half-closed eyes. If anyone was going to drown, it'd be Sunny.

Zach tried to climb on top of me, hoping for rescue, while I watched poor Sunny sink lower into the water. I pushed Zach off and headed toward shore so Sunny would turn and follow me. I hadn't noticed Sadie had found a way better stick than the one I had thrown. She was barely able to wrap her jaws around it and it was nearly five feet long. Within a minute or so, she was right behind me. I got out of her way, but she hit Zach smack on the head. I grabbed him and reached Sunny before she knocked him out.

Sadie made it to shore, dropped the stick and barked at me to throw it so she could do it all over again. The two boys didn't move but sat shivering in the hot sun. I don't think they ever went back in the water.

* * *

Sunny's medical problems flared up again when he was around thirteen years old. If the previous owner hadn't put his age at five-years-old on the surrender papers, I would have guessed younger. At thirteen, he was still energetic, ready to run with me on the Poudre Trail, still in love with Sadie and a tad more courageous around Zach, not scurrying off my bed anymore when Zach jumped up looking for a fight. My body was the DMZ every night, neither dog crossing over, careful to keep legs and heads in their own territory. Zach preferred under the covers near the crook of my knees, while I hugged Sunny to my belly. We both liked it.

He must have eaten something bad, I thought, because a couple of days before New Year's Eve, he stopped eating and began vomiting. Then he seemed okay. But I knew better. He had swallowed something which turned out to be a slick goose-poop covered rock. I knew the signs of an abdominal obstruction well. Sixteen years ago, Jake had died of one and the hunching of the spine and sorrowful eyes spoke of an unbearable pain.

My vet had retired for good and the vet who bought her practice admitted she wasn't good at abdominal surgeries. I called around and found Dr. Tim. It was December 31, 2015. He did the surgery immediately and I was grateful. But he didn't keep his surgical patients overnight, and I would have to bring him to the Emergency Care Hospital down the street, so they could watch him for the next twenty-four hours. He suggested I transport him since it would save me money.

I picked up my little Sunny boy from Dr. Tim's, wrapped in a warm blanket, tucked him into the passenger seat of my old Subaru and drove in a blinding snowstorm the three miles to the hospital. I stayed with him for an hour, to make sure he was sedated and at ease, then had to leave unless I wanted to spend the night sprawled out on uncomfortable plastic chairs, my car no longer able to navigate the three feet of snow that would eventually cover the streets.

No matter that Sunny was still a jerk, still peed on the side of my bed, the leather couch, my Treadmill and any box, suitcase, or large purse left carelessly unprotected—I sobbed all the way home. My only experience with abdominal surgery had ended in sepsis and death. I thought I was losing him.

New Year's Day dawned crisp and sunny, and the roads were soon clear. I took my time that morning, acknowledging having two dogs was an exponential difference from three. The quiet was deeper and my antennae, normally on high alert, listening for an intake of breath, a snort, a rapid clicking of canine toenails, was relaxed. The hospital had called me at five in the morning when they did rounds, to tell me Sunny had taken an hour or so to fully fall asleep. He had cried, though not loud enough to wake the other patients. He would be ready to go home at ten. They said he missed me.

"He needs his mommy," they said when I got there. Within a few days, he was eating and pooping. The surgery and overnight care cost me two thousand dollars. I had been putting away cash, hidden in my closet for the time when my sixteen-year-old Subaru Outback would finally die. The next day I bought pet insurance for all three dogs.

Nearly a year passed when Sunny started throwing up again, not eating and hunched over. The only thing the vet found in the x-ray and ultrasound was a collection of strictures which were a result of scar tissue in the small intestine. It was December 31, 2016, another New Year's Eve spent waiting to hear if Sunny would die.

This time, the vet took out sections of the intestine which weren't allowing food to pass and were causing a blockage. I took him home that night and slept with him on his bed, so he wouldn't cry. So, this is how he was going to go, I concluded. Not this year, maybe not next. But this is how Sunny would die.

The following summer he had surgery to remove his left eye because of glaucoma. He also went deaf. In July, Sunny started up with the abdominal symptoms again and I rushed him to Emergency Care Hospital before ten o'clock p.m. when the rates went up. He spent the night, but whatever was stuck had passed and he was home with me the next evening.

* * *

I was Zach's last victim, though I use the term 'victim' loosely. It's a story I tell reluctantly, my only defense being that I had no idea he was suffering so from degenerative disc disease and that his recent odd gait was a result of pinched nerves and compromised discs. He was in severe pain. Just before bed, I reached for Zach and kissed him on the neck as he lay ensconced between my two bed pillows. His reaction was swift and painful. He bit me in the throat and drew blood. I hit him and called him a shithead. Not hard, he was just a little thing, but hard enough that he jumped off the bed and landed hunched and terrified.

"I'm so sorry!" I was in tears and shocked at my violence. He had been my constant companion for twelve years and I still didn't know him. Or me. He ran into the living room and snuggled up to Sadie, who had by then, started spending the night in the big bed meant for Great Danes or my threesome who infrequently slept together, curled up, spine-to-spine and butt-to-butt. I could tell he didn't want me to pick him up. I lay on the floor, a few feet from him and Sadie, and cried. He would never have done that to me if something weren't wrong. I begged for his forgiveness. It took a while, but he soon allowed me to pick him up and take him back to my bed where we both lay, a little more afraid of each other.

It was a couple weeks later that he tried to get up from one of the doggie beds and couldn't. He had an appointment for another dental cleaning in a few days and I waited for that to also do an X ray on his spine. I don't know why I waited. My 'wait-n-see' attitude was stupid.

People had come over for my birthday party and Sarah

brought her two-year-old and three-year-old, warily. She didn't trust my little terriers who I had to hide in my bedroom for most of the party. After everyone left, I brought out the dogs and started cleaning up. Zach didn't join Sunny or Sadie in the kitchen, sniffing around for dropped globs of guacamole. I headed back to the living room and checked on him.

"Hey, buddy, what's up? What are you doing?"

Zach tried to get up and slowly fell back.

I knew then that I would be losing Zach. It was too late to save him, but I tried anyway, first with laser therapy, some acupuncture then ultrasound treatment, then finally I had X-rays and an ultrasound diagnosis that showed he was suffering terribly with no good permanent solution at hand.

At first, we thought it was a soft tissue injury, but it got worse even with treatment and pain meds. He began to howl everyday around four in the morning. and I couldn't pick him up unless I used a towel and held my arms out stiff, so I could keep his spine straight. Within a couple of weeks, he stopped being able to go out and pee with any steadiness.

I remembered Becca and Jesse and how blind and deaf I was to their pain and suffering. Never again ... was what I said. Sitting outside the Four Seasons Emergency and Radiology Clinic, a referral from my vet, I knew Zach and I were both done for. He looked better, I thought to myself. He's standing with just a little wobbling. He was trying to make it all better. So was I, unable to negotiate this territory.

"It's gonna be okay, right buddy? Just a few more days maybe and some more drugs, we'll beat it, right?" I refused to cry. Zach was hunched over, protecting his neck and his lower back, his tail wagging back and forth.

On the way home, I called my vet and asked about an at-home euthanasia. Sunny and Sadie had to be there, and I wanted to make it calm and peaceful for Zach.

I played a chant from my old Kundalini yoga classes, lit

incense and the fireplace. Zach laid on his side on the big bed in the middle of the living room, following me with his eyes as Sadie paced up and down the hallway, uncharacteristically ill at ease. Sunny sat in Zach's crate where I had kept Zach when I had to leave the house during the last few weeks, so he didn't move too much and hurt himself worse.

We had been a team, the four of us the last nine years, and Zach and me and Sadie for eleven years. Zach was the youngest, just a kid at twelve-years old. Rat terriers live forever, I'm told, as do toy fox terriers and Chihuahua mixes. They lied, somebody lied. I leaned over Zach and whispered that he should find out who they were and bite them.

The vet came with his assistant, and they entered our space with reverence and, I think, a little sadness. He had only been Zach's vet for a couple of years after our vet had retired, but those years had been filled with too many vet visits, trauma and an overwrought human unable to face the loss of her charges.

The music changed to a Buddhist chant *Om Mani Padme Hum,* a chant I use when I see roadkill or a car accident. And I used to sing it to Zach when "You Are my Sunshine" no longer worked. It is said that all the Buddhist teaching is wrapped up in this one chant. It is untranslatable into English and has to do with helping us connect to our innate compassion.

Maybe the vet and his assistant felt the sacredness in the room that night. I know it was there and I did the best I could to honor Zach, but all I felt was grief and loss and shame that I didn't recognize his pain earlier. I promised Sadie and Sunny I wouldn't do that to them.

I wish I could say I kept that promise.

CHAPTER 13

MAZZY

2006-2022

W hen Cody, the future-husband, came into Sarah's life, Toby didn't take long to accept him. A couple years later, they would adopt Mazzy, another shepherd mix, and just a kid at one year old. She loved Toby with the adoration of an adolescent in love with a boy band.

I include Mazzy in this book for the same reason I included Toby. I'm their grandmother and they gave me their loyalty and affection when their mom and dad weren't around. They also spent many a night sleeping on my bed or in close vicinity.

Toby was Mazzy's god, though at times he would snap at

her to leave him alone. I remember moments when Mazzy would lie down near Toby and watch him as if waiting for orders, but I think she just wanted him to love her.

Mazzy is a beautiful shepherd mix, long and tall where Toby was wider and more powerful. Sometimes I watch Mazzy from a distance, and I think—"Now, that's a coyote." With her light brown head and teepee-shaped ears, her tapered, lean body with a bushy tail and long legs, she could be mistaken for an aging coyote matriarch.

Sarah and Cody may have regretted adopting Mazzy in the beginning. Her separation anxiety was powerful and mighty and dictated how they planned their day. She tore apart her wire crate, jumped on a glass table and destroyed it, ripped holes through doors and howled with the vigor of an animal in pain.

Both were in law school and neither wanted to be the first one home, reluctant to face a frantic or wounded or dead Mazzy, and the aftermath of a massive panic attack. Even the love of Toby couldn't alleviate Mazzy's fear. It eventually lessened and the two dogs settled in, content and happy with each other's company. Especially Mazzy.

I took care of both dogs whenever Sarah and Cody needed me to. I also had three terriers and my house became a kennel, dog beds spread everywhere, dog bowls in different rooms. Sadie was known to wander to the other dogs' dinners and command them to step aside. They all did, even Toby. But Sadie and Toby were old friends and I imagine she was Toby's first love, if dog's have first love. I'd like to think so.

Mazzy and Sadie were friends, too, but for much of their friendship, Mazzy stood wary of Sadie's swagger. Sadie chased Mazzy from one end of the yard to the other—a speedy little ten-pound toy fox terrier intent on catching Mazzy's lustrous tail, wanting Mazzy to chase her back. There were two other small dogs in the yard—Zach and Sunny—

and their efforts to befriend Mazzy were half-hearted at best. I imagine she intimidated them with their nearly fifty-pound weight difference, but if either of the boys had been even a little welcoming, Mazzy might have relaxed a bit around them.

When Mazzy stays with me now, we're inseparable. Even with Frida here. Room-to-room, Mazzy wanders and finds another empty bed to occupy while I cook, or go to the bathroom, work on my computer, and finally sleep. She can't jump on the bed anymore but takes the bed stairs carefully and lies over my legs and closes her eyes. I move eventually, not willing to risk having my blood supply cut off, but she never adjusts her own position. She's there for the night.

Mazzy always wants our attention. She nuzzles, whines a little and attempts to leap up to make sure we see her. She kisses incessantly; her persistence is irritating. Toby accepted affection when he felt like it. He didn't always feel like it, getting up and moving to a different spot when the fawning over him became too much. But he always allowed Mazzy to lay beside him for comfort and companionship, licking him occasionally to show her love.

I saw Toby for the last time just after Sarah and Cody welcomed little Lulu, their first child. Toby had the typical hip issues and was taking Rimadyl and arthritis supplements. I remember standing in their kitchen and looking at him lying in his bed, unhappy and in pain, or so I thought. Sarah said he was doing okay. I disagreed, I thought he was struggling.

I went home to Fort Collins from their place near City Park in Denver. I got the call at three in the morning. They were rushing Toby to the vet, prepared for him to get exploratory surgery to see what was going on. They didn't need it. Toby died shortly after getting there from a burst tumor. I headed down the next morning to an inconsolable Sarah holding a tiny baby who had just met her first dog. Both Cody and Sarah struggled through the day, caring for a baby, and dealing with Toby's death. He was only eleven, young in our eyes.

Sarah compares her next three dogs to Toby as if he were a Super Dog—intelligent, trained, gorgeous, protective yet gentle with babies and kittens. The illusion slowly dissipated, and we'd remember Toby never coming when called unless he was headed in our direction, anyway. He was smart but intractable and could never be off leash. But he *was* gorgeous and sometimes we'd sit around and stare at him.

My favorite photo of Toby is a full-on portrait of his head, sprinkled in snow, somewhere out in the mountains, his eyes steady and clear, a dog who'd follow you to the ends of the earth. And you'd do the same for him.

A few weeks after Toby died, Cody asked me if I had any photos of Toby.

"Sure, quite a few, for some reason." I asked if he was creating The Book of Toby.

He said yes, and it would be beautiful. And it was.

The cover was my favorite photo of him, covered in snow and looking like he ruled the world.

When Mazzy lost Toby, her nudges for attention became more insistent, more resolute as she shoved her long nose into someone's crotch, a move guaranteed to get results, though not always the one she wanted.

When Sarah and Cody run, Mazzy is unstoppable, matching them stride-by-stride, never wanting to stop. Sometimes they run long—maybe six or seven miles—and I think it was too much, but for Mazzy, it was pure joy.

By this time, Sarah had Lou or Lulu, quickly followed by Theo, and her patience grew thin. Mazzy must step aside for a while. But not for long. The babies, then toddlers, hug her clumsily, fall on her and sleep in the curve of her belly. She still looks up at Sarah and smiles when one of the kids flops down for a tight hug around Mazzy. She was born to do this.

I worry, of course. Photos on Facebook show babies curled on top of dogs who are showing warning signs, ears back, tongues hanging out, cowering. I expect the next Facebook post to be the one that says the dog attacked their baby and they had to put their dog down because they were stupid.

But that's not Mazzy. I believe all my dogs, and everyone else's dog, could become aggressive if aggravated enough, but not Mazzy. Despite her anxiety as a younger dog and the loss of her beloved Toby, Mazzy is here to accept and give love, annoying as that can be.

When I visit my daughter and her family, Mazzy is waiting at the door, whining for me to sit with her and kiss and hug. She used to jump up on me, but it's become difficult for her. Her hips are arthritic, she had a cruciate ligament tear just a couple years ago, and she's been diagnosed with canine myelopathy. It's a loss of myelin, the white matter sheathing the spinal cord. Sort of a doggie MS.

She's twelve years old now, but just as willing to speed around a campsite, go for a short jog, climb up and down stairs following the grandkids on another adventure, and snuggle in bed with Sarah and Cody. I'm honored she chooses me to sleep with when I spend the night.

The specter of her looming death hangs lightly when I'm visiting Sarah and Cody's house. A month ago, Cody took Mazzy with him for his annual camping and fishing trip with his friends. He let Mazzy have the run of the place as she leapt from one tree to another, one gross smell to another, skirting the edge of the lake, never quite willing to throw herself in the water but eager to disrupt the serious fly-fishing. No one cared. She remembers her past, her way past as a wolf, and she looks like one disappearing in the woods for minutes at a time, maybe more. Cody lets her. He knows she'll be back. And she does return, limping and exhausted before she settles by the fire.

Every dog should have this. Every dog should feel the freedom to stretch their muscles and minds, remembering that their ancestors once roamed these lands. I think about my spoiled dogs and laugh. If I had let them free in the woods, would they have disappeared up gullies or into caves or skittered through lakes and rivers and over mountains? Sadie for certain. But I'd lose her to a hungry bear or coyote willing to engage in a fight with a pissed off ten-pound terrier, baring what was left of her teeth, punching the air on her hind legs, fully acknowledging this would be her last stand. My terrier boys would beat me to the car.

Mazzy always comes back. She has a fierce love for her humans and would never consider abandoning them to a world without her loyalty and love.

But that time will come, and I fear it.

Mazzy had a seizure on New Year's Eve 2021 and passed the next day, January 1, 2022—at home surrounded by her family. She leaves behind everyone, but especially my daughter's new dog Creek who is inconsolable, even three months later.

* * *

Over the next few months after Zach's death, Sadie limped more often and had more episodes where she couldn't walk for a few minutes, her knee dislocating and not slipping back into place.

Unfortunately, her speed demon runs, stops, and turns aggravated her luxating patella, where the kneecap moves out of its natural position. The only thing I was told to do was to not let her run off leash. I blame myself for not researching more, for not looking for other opinions or supplements or exercise I could have done with her. Her breed was part of the problem, prone to patella issues, but I could have done more. I see now there are many useful products and exercises that would have strengthened the adjoining muscles. Underwater treadmills and teaching her the army crawl, laughable for Sadie. She was a smart dog who easily learned tricks, but she had her pride.

Instead, I'd leash them up and we'd run, then walk, the bike paths near the Poudre River. Over time, other walkers, runners, and bikers recognized the woman with three terriers on leash, zigzagging on the path, her three dogs barely under control. But I never saw Sadie as happy as she was at the ponds, running free, chasing whatever little critter had the bad luck to be in the way, or dragging back to shore an unwieldy stick, poking her fellow canines in the eye.

I had Sadie for sixteen years, her presence steady and comforting without being intrusive. When she died, I felt I had lost an extra limb, not crucial to my existence, but stunning in its loss.

Her death came suddenly. She had stopped eating and was retching foam. I put off the ultrasound a couple of days to see if it was just temporary indigestion. She stopped drinking. Later that day she paced for nearly an hour outside where she'd sway as if buffeted by winds on a quiet night in March, just months before her sixteenth birthday, a day I planned to celebrate with human friends, doggie friends, and my own homemade doggie treats.

I couldn't get into Four Seasons, the ultrasound place, until two o'clock in the afternoon. I could've gone earlier, but I had an appointment with a client I thought was important. It wasn't. I was being selfish. This is where I beat myself up like any self-respecting dog lover would. It's why I hesitate in getting more dogs. I should have gone earlier, found out the truth and allowed her to pass peacefully, just in time to join the pack running the ponds or wherever dogs go when they die.

The radiologist told me she had acute pancreatitis and at her age, any attempts to cure her would be painful and most likely, unsuccessful. Instead of allowing her to pass then, I took her home and walked around the house and my yard while I held her close in a warm blanket. I called a friend who had spent years as a vet tech. I had made an appointment with my vet to put Sadie down. The earliest he could do it was the next day at five o'clock.

My friend was adamant. No more waiting. Let's find a place still open. By now, it was after six. I met her at an emergency vet open until eleven o'clock. The first injection allowed Sadie to relax and slide slowly down onto the table as I held her. I could tell her pain was gone, and she looked at me with what I hoped was gratitude. After she was gone, I went over to pick up her body and take it home with me. I hadn't gone anywhere without her for sixteen years. It was instinct. My friend placed her hand on my arm and said, "They'll take care of her."

That's *my* job, I wanted to say. I hesitated, trying to understand this would be the last time I would ever see her. I stared hard at her tiny body for a few seconds, asked for her forgiveness for the hundredth time and left.

It was after her Sadie's death when I remembered how I told my daughter she would have to care for Sadie when I was dead because Sadie was immortal. There were countless times she should have fallen twenty or more feet from a tree or suffered accidents which may have ended another dog's life. Or been lost, crossed major streets alone, attacked big snakes that slithered away instead of retaliating, encountered big dogs who didn't appreciate her Little Big Dog attitude. I was convinced I would die before she did, and made my daughter promise to care for her when I finally left this world.

But I had to first tell the story of Sadie's origins; why I

bought a dog at a pet store. In 2010, I co-founded a nonprofit dedicated to educating the world about puppy mills and their connection with pet stores. The truth had to come out. But I was still deeply anxious about public speaking and my stuttering. I started with Toastmasters, then heard about Ignite Fort Collins, where the speakers had well-rehearsed speeches timed with twenty slides which moved every fifteen seconds. There would be at least five hundred people in the audience. There was no room to screw up. This was my big chance to tell the sorrowful story about puppy mills and what we can all do to combat their existence.

The day came and I gave the speech. People wept and clapped, and I was happy. A kid even told me afterwards they were just about to buy a puppy from Pet City, a local pet store, but instead, they were adopting from a rescue.

I had made a difference! I came home to Sadie and told her everything and she blinked and went back to sleep. Her disinterest in my personal life had never deterred me before, so I thanked her for inspiring me to get up on stage and speak for her and millions of other dogs who were still suffering at puppy mills, but mainly I thanked her for being the catalyst that got me to speak again and to keep finding opportunities to speak. I said I'd hope she'd continue her inspirational ways after I died. I told her she was magical and would live forever.

I came to see Sadie as the hub that held our tribe together, both humans and dogs. She was the one constant, the one who ruled the house, the land, and any water we happened to be near. A dog trainer would admonish me for giving up my natural role, but I just thought she was better at it. She was there to welcome five different dogs, to say goodbye to three of them, she watched as a six-year relationship failed, when both kids left for college, when Sarah got married and had two kids, when I moved, when I started and finished my master's degree and when I applied for Social Security and Medicare.

Sadie was my conscience—a walking, eating, barking, swimming, pooping manifestation of my own inner judge. Maybe if I had listened to her a few times, my life may have been different. It would certainly have been less chaotic. She may have cautioned against accepting Zach into the fold though they did become close friends. She would have never welcomed Sunny. She didn't like Dylan for a long time and if it had been up to her, Dylan would've been just a weekend guest. But he was good to her, and she would have missed out on the gift of a kind male presence. As would I.

When I search Pefinder.com for other dogs, I realize I'm looking for another Sadie. Improbable, I know. But not impossible.

* * *

Five months after Sadie's death, Sunny wouldn't sleep with me. Instead, he found comfort in the closet on my Zabuton, the pad I put under my meditation cushion, to ease the discomfort of my feet and ankles. Each of my dogs had chosen that place just before they died. Sunny rose and hurried out to the kitchen where he violently threw up. Then he did it again in the sunroom before I reached the doggie door to get him outside.

It was two in the morning and I had promised my daughter I would head down to Broomfield to hang out with her and the kids. I calculated what time I could text her and tell her I couldn't come. I thought about who else would want to know. I left a message with Dr. Tim around five, making sure I would be the first call his receptionist would return when she got in that morning.

There would be no surgery. Sunny was fifteen years old and I wouldn't put him through that again. Nor would I put me through it, either. Dr. Tim recommended I get an ultrasound at the same place I had taken Sadie just a few months prior, "Just in case."

"Just in case" it was nothing? "Just in case" it was simple indigestion or a bad piece of whatever unknown substance he had inhaled the night before? I knew better, but it seemed right that Sunny would be diagnosed at the same vet clinic that told me Zach had pinched nerves and was wracked by severe disc degeneration and that Sadie had acute pancreatitis. They got me in immediately. I knew what was coming and texted my son in New Orleans, my sister, Nancy, and Buddhist brother, Billy, who would perform some chants for Sunny.

The radiologist was kind and thorough, showing me a large obstruction and what she thought may have been bowel cancer or necrosis.

"He's in terrible pain, Mary. You could take him to your vet and make him comfortable until he's able to euthanize him— or you could do it now. In the next room. It's comfortable and quiet and you can have as much time as you want."

She was right, of course. But I wasn't ready. Sunny and I were a team now, just the two of us. I took him everywhere and he walked steady and calm on the Poudre Trail. Finally. It felt good and normal and how it was supposed to be with our dogs. He slept a lot but was always ready to go with me anywhere even if it meant waiting in the car patiently while I got coffee for me and a few dog treats at Poudre Feed and Supply next store. We had spent the summer wading in the Poudre River and walking in the early morning while the streets were still cool to the touch and the grass was wet from the morning dew.

I talked about what happened in the last few months, about his affection for Sadie, and how upset he was when we had to say goodbye to Zach in my living room. I wish he could have told me how he felt, lying in Zach's crate, his legs across the entry way, his head held high, watching as Zach slipped away in that gigantic dog bed. Sunny had whined then and every bad opinion I had of him vanished. I saw him as a compassionate being, misunderstood and suffering, I suppose like the lot of humanity.

I lay on a blanket on the floor with Sunny and held him like we were back in my bed. His coat was shedding like crazy, and I laughed when the vet tech asked me if I wanted a snip of his hair. My clothes were covered in Sunny's yellow, prickly fur, as was my car, my yoga mat, meditation cushion, the corners of the house, the heating vents, under the sofa cushions and on every piece of clothing hanging in my closet. She smiled and left, closing the door reverently.

I told Sunny how much I loved him and what a *very, very* good dog he was, and how much I'll miss him—sleeping on my bed, riding in the car, walking the Poudre Trail. His pain was obvious, he was suffering, I had to let him go. Apologizing and crying, I pushed the button that would summon the guy with the needles and the drugs.

Again, I was surprised by the swiftness by which death comes. He was gone, but I stayed ten minutes or so, hugging him tight, still expressing my gratitude for his companionship and the laughter and silliness he brought to my life. He died August 24, 2017 and I didn't get my car cleaned until November 25th. The carwash guy stared at the yellow dog hairs free-floating through the interior, asking me how many damn dogs I had.

"None," I said. It felt weird.

"I'm not sure if we can get all this hair out unless we do a more detailed job," he looked at me funny.

"That's okay, a few dog hairs here and there never killed anybody."

CHAPTER 14
FRIDA

2018–

I doubt if I could physically hurt a human or any being. But I trust few and confess to fewer. I'm quick to misunderstand intentions. My first inclination isn't kind or loving. My heart is protected from harmful virus invaders like the sneeze guards at salad bars. Not just protecting, but deflecting the unwelcome hug, the arm around the shoulders, the admonishment to go on Match.com. In my wildest dreams, I can no longer imagine a man's embrace or declaration of love. I need at least five feet of distance between me and you and if you move closer, I'll run out the back door to see if the raccoons have slunk back into their culverts. As I write this, the country is social distancing because of COVID-19. I can relax.

I *want* to be different; I *want* to hang out with a circle of friends, share intimacies, be trusted and trust, say nice things to and about people, maybe even consider a coffee date. I just can't.

But the shield disappears when I see a dog. It can be any dog, really, but when I see Frida, her startling ears in full bloom, her front left leg slightly askew, a ballerina with one foot in turnout, the guard lifts and I feel delight like a child handed a raspberry-lime popsicle on a hot summer day.

It had been five months since Sunny died. And nearly thirty years since the last time I was dogless. Take your time, I said to myself. Wake up when *you* want, I thought. Go see Dan in New Orleans, spend a couple of nights with Sarah and the family in Broomfield. Spend a week at a writing retreat! I was getting excited.

My backyard could flourish again. Mulch and stone would respect each other's boundaries. The yellow spots would disappear. I could have people over. We could sip cocktails and play corn hole without stepping in a missed piece of dog poop. My car would stay free of dog hair as would my entire closet.

I gave myself a year to enjoy what normal people enjoy. Except I didn't know what that was. I didn't know how to walk in a room without picking up a dog and kissing it. Or making dinner without putting aside a little salmon skin and sweet potato. There were a bunch of little holes in my bed I couldn't fill no matter how much I stretched out. I had no one to talk to while driving around town looking for free puppacinos. I started walking the trails faster and for longer, not tied to two old dogs in a dog jogger and one lazy one on leash. But too many people stopped me to ask where the pups were.

It was too painful. I biked instead and flew past anyone before they recognized me.

I began a casual search on Petfinder.com about five months after Sunny died. I saw a cute little terrier and went to see her. I didn't bring a leash. I just wanted to see how it would feel to get attached again, to be vulnerable to another fifteen-pound lunatic.

The house was in a town about twenty minutes away out in the country. There were two women at the house, one who was running a day care along with her dog fostering duties and her friend who specialized in fostering pregnant dog moms. She also brought along Wynter in case I didn't like Belle.

Belle was a ten-pound lunatic and not in a good way. She ran after Wynter and tried to bite her, yapping and growling. I specified I needed a dog good with little kids. Wynter was gorgeous and seemed stunned by Belle's aggression. When she jumped in my lap, trying to escape Belle's efforts to disembowel her, I knew she was coming home with me. I pretended she wasn't, but no one was fooled by my nonchalance.

"How old is she?" I asked. Not that it mattered. I was going home alone.

"She has babies, too?" Not that I cared. I didn't want a puppy even if it *was* supernaturally cute.

"She was an amazing mom?" Why should that be relevant? She couldn't babysit my grandkids.

Twenty minutes later, I was walking out of the house with a borrowed leash and a folder with Frida's paperwork. I had already picked out a name for my next dog.

Frida is braver than I am, inching closer to people who stop to admire her exquisiteness. She stretches her neck forward, relying on her nose to make her decisions, poised to jump back if they reach down to pet her too soon. A kind and knowing person will sit and wait for Frida to decide if the person is worthy of her attention. Smart girl. Smarter than me, according to Laura, the trainer I hired right after Frida killed that mouse.

Laura gives her clients the side-eye. The owners, not the

dogs. Like me, she's from Boston and I understand her brusqueness and inclination to think her human clients decorate the truth. Laura's skeptical of dog owners who say they *want* to train their dogs. We really don't. It's a lie. We want our dogs to read our minds and act accordingly.

Frida and I met her at the end of my driveway to see if Frida could join her and the ten dogs inside the van on all-day adventure hikes.

"You got to make her stop." Laura looked at me as Frida barked at the van-load of potential friends and enemies. I shrugged my shoulders and smiled. What can I do? Laura walked over, took the leash, and shushed Frida who wagged her tail then sat quietly.

"Good girl, Frida," Laura smiled. The two of them headed down the street with Laura giving commands.

"Turn. Heel. Stop."

I don't know this dog. She performs as if she was competing in Obedience Trials as the dog to beat. Laura brings over one dog at a time for Frida to sniff and for them to sniff her. Lots of tail-wagging and play bows.

"She can come. How about Friday?"

I nodded yes. Laura leaned down to tell Frida goodbye. then drove off with her motley tribe.

"What the hell was that?" I stared at Frida. She had never responded to any request of mine. For a moment I regretted not getting a goofy golden retriever mix or a loyal, steadfast yellow lab. Terriers were exasperating, wily and couldn't be trusted.

Back in the yard, she looked back at me from her rock throne, smelling the liver treats in my hand. I called her over. She didn't hesitate. Someday she'll come without me waving foul-smelling bits of what looks like bear poop.

"What a good girl," I smiled at her, as she sits, her front paws tip-tapping on the grass in anticipation. I took a picture of the yard with my phone and uploaded it to Facebook with the words, "Frida loves me so much she takes all my stuff outside and plays with it!" For a moment I hesitated, knowing my trainer will see I have handed over the keys to the kingdom to Frida. I shrugged my shoulders and clicked 'post.'

Frida looked tiny on the extra-large dog bed I bought a few years earlier from Costco. Hundreds of dog beds had lined the aisle back then and I went a little crazy, buying this gigantic bed and a few smaller ones to scatter about the house in case any of my pups felt the need to nap alone, away from the madding crowd, as it were.

I also had fantasies of my three terriers curled up together, nose to butt, best pals for life, sleeping peacefully in the middle of the largest dog bed I'd ever seen. It happened a few times and I took an enormous number of photos as evidence, then posted the visual proof on Facebook just in case I lost my phone and never figured out how to access my photos from the cloud. When my dogs died, I tossed out a couple of the more disgusting beds and threw the cover of the big one in the washing machine turned to the Sanitizing option.

Frida laid unfurled in the middle of it, barely creating a dent. She reminded me of Sadie, except she's longer and has better hearing. Sadie was nearly deaf at the end of her life and I forgot how sharp a young dog's hearing can be. When I tried to sneak up on Frida to take an adorable photo, Frida's eyes snapped open, her ears turning in my direction. She's part bat and can hear ground movement and when my breathing changes.

It was Frida's third bout with mastitis and antibiotics weren't working. She might have had the infection when I adopted her. I woke up to our first morning together with blood on the top of my quilt and on my arm where I had hugged Frida. I was supposed to go to the second Women's March after Trump's 2016 election but made a frantic call to my friends to say I would be at the vet's all morning and they should leave without me. The vet treated the infection, but it returned, and a mass of tissue kept growing despite treatment.

My vet wanted to reassure me he doesn't always solve problems with surgery. He was the vet I went to when Sunny had his first abdominal surgery and when Zach and Sadie had infected teeth and required emergency oral surgery. Sunny was back again a year later to have his eye removed and then surgery to remove the strictures which had formed in his small intestine from the previous surgery. I agreed to have Frida's mass removed.

"Frida did great," the vet said. He always said that. I wondered what it would mean if he said she didn't do well. Death? Coma? Brain damage? After I listened to the care instructions, Frida and I walked outside with a couple of the vet techs who opened my car door as I carefully picked her up and placed her on the towel in the back seat. She whimpered.

Both vet techs cooed back, "Poor girl!"

"Her IV with the pain meds is wearing off. Give her the Tramadol and Rimadyl as soon as you get home," one of the techs reached in and stroked her on the muzzle. I thanked them and drove off.

After a small meal and a pee, Frida went straight to the big bed. She didn't move until I got up to make some food and returned with a plate of chicken, brown rice, and asparagus. She got up, staggering a little but didn't let a little pain and confusion stop her from begging.

"Here you go, baby girl," I said, handing her a slice of chicken from my plate. It's a no-no but it wouldn't be the first time I'd given her food from my dinner in the seven months I had Frida. At the moment, I didn't care that I was unraveling all the training we'd done together. She was hurting. I'd do anything to make her happy again.

Frida wobbled back to her bed and was asleep in seconds. Her snore was barely audible, but it was sweet, and I quietly moved closer to her, watching her eyelids flutter and her nose twitch. She was still deep in a drugged sleep and couldn't hear me. The vet warned me about the length of the incision and the number of stitches, but it still surprised me. The cut traveled from under her right armpit down her right side, ending just past the big brown heart-shaped spot. Part of the heart was now shaved off, the right ventricle to be precise.

I've never had serious medical issues with a dog during our first year together. I had also never adopted a mother. All signs pointed to Frida being a breeder dog from a puppy mill during the Houston 2017 floods. Mill owners aren't known for their attention to their dogs' health and Frida had most likely never seen a vet. I assumed Frida escaped the mill during the Houston storms and had wandered the streets, pregnant and hungry, for a few weeks. But she was a terrier, predatory and skilled in killing. I imagined she wasn't hungry for long.

Despite her conjectured past, Frida is an excellent dog. She's a smart and stubborn eighteen-month-old Chihuahua, Jack Russell Terrier, maybe Corgi mix, white with large fawn-colored, heart-shaped spots on each side of her body that match the color of her eyes, as if somebody gave her appearance a lot of thought. She holds up the long curving tail of a Chihuahua and her ears—Yoda-like, huge and commanding—face forward, alert to an errant squirrel or snake invading her territory. Quick and lithe, she has already killed baby rabbits and at least five snakes. Karmically, Frida's probably doomed, but it's her nature and I can't change that.

I've never been able to change any of my dog's natures. Training could have helped a few of them, but I gave up trying to wrangle terriers a long time ago.

People are another thing. We should be able to change, after all. We're supposed to be more self-aware, more practiced in the art of self-reflection. We have knowledge, access to tools like therapy, meditation, Twelve Step Programs, but change for most of us, is incremental, minuscule in our attempt to become better or at least less offensive people. A good dog trainer would go a long way for some of us.

Frida's affectionate, confident, and listens to me about fifty percent of the time. I'm hopeful the percentage will increase. Laura, the trainer, insists I don't let her run the yard free without a long leash until her 'recall' is perfect. In my head, I laugh a little while trying to keep a straight face. She's right, of course, and it's annoying when Frida sits ten feet from me and refuses to come when called. I'm supposed to use 'high value' treats and call her once. If she doesn't come, I tug on the leash. I'm supposed to do this until she comes immediately then take off the leash and keep practicing. I will never do this, or at least I'll never do this consistently. Her 'recall' skills, or my 'recall' skills will never be perfect.

When Frida had knee surgery, all training is abandoned, and I do anything for her and excuse any behavior.

But before that happened, I bought her hundreds of dollars' worth of treats, expensive food, leashes, and toys. I also spent money on dog training classes, despite my continued failures, and doggie daycare. Twice a month she headed up to Red Feather Lakes in the mountains with ten of her best canine friends and her trainer and spends the day hiking without me. I scouted the better dog parks and made sure our walks were always at different parts of the city, so she doesn't get bored. She loves to play, and I arranged play dates, not ready to start building a bigger dog family just yet.

I learned my lesson with Sunny and signed Frida up for pet health insurance the day she came home with me. It costs me sixty dollars a month. If I go somewhere overnight, I pay thirty dollars a day for her care. I don't like leaving her for more than three hours when I'm showing property, so I take her to one of the dog sitters I found on Rover.com. Years ago, when my kids were young and right after my divorce, I needed a job that paid more than subsistence living so I chose real estate because a friend talked me into it when I told her I wanted to be around for my kids after school. It's the same with Frida.

When I pick her up, I get a rundown of how her day went and if she took a light or hard nap. Earlier in the day, I received text photos of her back end or a blurry video of her running across the yard chasing her favorite canine friend. It makes me think about our childhood dog Taffy and how deprived she was —or how demented we've all gotten about our dogs. It reminded me of when I took my three-year-old daughter to preschool and they would hand me her 'artwork' when I picked her up. Frida thankfully doesn't have artwork.

Why do I do it? Why do any of us do it?

That's the question, isn't it?

* * *

I chuckle over what I wrote earlier in this book. Not that I stopped doing any of those things—knuckle bones from the butcher, looking for different trails, the best squeaky toys, but both daycare and hiking trips to Red Feather have stopped. I've slowed down on the treats, well, sort of, and she can come with me to my daughter Sarah's house, now that Sarah has confidence Frida won't rip her kids' faces off.

Recently, Frida caught a squirrel and snapped its neck, while I ran out the door screaming at her. I watched the squirrel die, his eyes slowly losing their light. I don't know if she wanted to eat it or play with it, but she barked at me to get out of the way. I didn't. She ran away, taunting me in my inability to catch her. I called out to my roommate to protect the dead squirrel from Frida while I fetched a shovel. Not all dogs would snap a squirrel's neck or try to eat it, but I excused Frida because she was alone and afraid and pregnant in the wilds of Houston just after the floods from Hurricane

Harvey. I rationalize she'll find us food when the Apocalypse comes.

Our walks are still in out-of-the-way places, especially near a body of water. Frida doesn't swim; she wades, slowly, tentatively sticking out her tongue to test the water. I encourage her to drink. It's early spring today but already seventy-eight degrees. She springs back on land; nervous I'm going to toss her in or get her wetter than she prefers.

Out of nowhere, a large black lab comes hurtling behind us and jumps, landing in the middle of the river. I'm afraid his enthusiasm for the water has terrified Frida, yet she loves big dogs and wants to go play. She must decide if her desire for the big goofy guy transcends her fear of the river. It does. I let her go as far as she wants. She's on a thirty-foot leash with an Easy Walk harness. It's safer and she can't squirm out of this harness like she did with my other ones.

A large plastic box in a storage area in my house holds all the dog paraphernalia I've bought over the years. None of the old harnesses quite suited Frida. The dog box is next to a box filled with my kids' artwork, compositions, and report cards. The dog box is bigger. I think it's because all the containers with my dead dog's ashes take up a lot of room as do their old food bowls.

I think about making a dog shrine with photos and leashes and name tags. A piece of art, maybe, or just honoring my canine friends. It's not a shrine to an idol like Elvis or an altar to honor the Buddha. It's something that will make me smile when I walk by. Occasionally, I'll give a piece of the shrine-to-be to my kids –a leash and a bowl for Sarah's new dog or Sunny's Doggles to Dan for when his dog rides on a boat.

My desire to construct this sacred space conflicts with my propensity for less crap. Hence, the big box stays closed.

Frida is frolicking in the water.

"Good girl, Frida," I shout, hoping she equates fun and play with water. The black lab does a little play bow, but his owner calls him, and they move on. Frida finds herself in the middle of the shallow river alone. She heads back to me, shakes, and walks back up the bank to the concrete bike path, eager to follow her new best friend.

None of my other terriers were friendly with dogs. Frida is a relief. I don't have to pull back on her leash when dogs sniff her butt and wag their tails. She wags back and play bows. My other terriers were jerks, acting like a dog gang from the 'hood,' claiming their territory (the entire world) or protecting their human (a joke). They'd never bite, but they'd snarl and growl and look ferocious. One time Sunny barked incessantly at a scared little puppy, terrifying its owner when I accidentally dropped his leash. When Sunny realized he was no longer being held back, he turned and ran back to me and slunk between my legs. Zach did the same thing. Neither of them was brave in any interpretation of the word. Sadie enjoyed the chase but never bit or fought another dog, though I could never trust this motley crew to not surround another dog and bully it into submission while its owner dialed Larimer Humane, the local 'dogcatcher.'

Frida makes me smile more than I realize. Despite her issues with recall and making me chase her around the yard, she's almost perfect. It's my fault, anyway, that she has a loose acquaintance with obedience training. It's never been my strength. I think I did better with bigger dogs, they weren't life-long babies I could scoop up and sing to while nuzzling them. And it takes time and patience with these strong-willed terriers. I vacillate between trying to be the tough guy and afraid they will hate me while I discipline them. I should probably never have a dog, but I'm aware of my limitations and try not to inflict my dogs' anti-social behavior on others.

But Frida's not like that. She may not come immediately

when called, but that's only because she's having fun or killing something. It's not good, I know. I'll keep trying.

* * *

Another six months have passed, and Frida is in her fifth week of rehab from knee surgery. My vet had recommended surgery for her luxating patella and warned if not addressed, she could tear her cruciate ligament.

Money had been tight the last few months, my real estate career on the down slide the past couple of years, coincidentally, in step with writing this book. I could pay for Frida's surgery, thanks to pet insurance, but it was still a few hundred dollars and an enormous amount of my time would be spent taking her to rehab and out to the yard on leash while she does her business.

Sadie had a luxating patella, an ailment common to these little Chihuahua mixes. It's basically a knee dislocation, the thigh unable to hold the kneecap in position. Sometimes a dog can lift the affected leg to stretch then relax the quadriceps muscles which pulls the patella back into place. I'm sure that's how Sadie avoided surgery, but she didn't wrestle furiously with a forty-pound puppy either. Frida did.

Sarah's dog Creek is young, strong, and playful, and it's non-stop brawling from the time Frida arrives at their house to when we leave. Both dogs jump from couch to chair to dog bed to playroom then out the door. Sarah and I think it's funny and good for the dogs to have a buddy. Sometimes Frida doesn't want to leave and resists walking out the door after I kiss my grandkids goodbye and try to go home. She fights the tug of the leash on her harness and slides across the floor, shoulders hunched, attempting to squirm out of her harness and continue the play date long into the night. I pick her up and put her in her car seat where she quietly whines for a few minutes.

She misses Creek and Mazzy, Sarah's older dog, I assume, but in retrospect, she's most likely in pain.

I had put off the surgery twice and it annoyed my vet. Maybe rehab and rest would take care of the issue, I hoped. After getting a second opinion of a vet that specialized in rehab, I capitulated. Frida had a partial cruciate tear and coupled with a luxating patella, there was only one option.

It wasn't just about the money, although finances are always a concern. I didn't want Frida to go under the knife. It could go sideways; she could get arthritis like I did, and I couldn't spend two months doing rehab with her—I could barely do that for me. She could also die.

My own issues with my knee and elbow from the high school car accident have worsened with age. Intellectually, I know I'll be in physical therapy or some healing body modality for the rest of my life, but it's an old story. I quit running, kickboxing, Zumba, most dancing, and any steep hikes. How is it going to be any different for Frida?

So, I got a doggie backpack, for me to carry her when she falters and can no longer walk along the Poudre Trail I must commune with daily. She's too heavy after fifteen minutes. My neck and lower back hurt and I spent the evening in spasm. Finally, I bought a used Burley combination bike trailer/kid jogger which is as easy to use as a stroller even along the dirt paths of the ponds just east of town. She walks until she can't, and I scoop her up and clip her into the stroller where she sits regally, her ears forward and alert, looking like the Queen she is.

People smiled as I strode past, making comments about how their dog would love to be pushed along. Sometimes I say she's injured, later I say she's rehabbing after the surgery. Mostly, I think it's an inane comment and no self-respecting dog would want to be pushed along a path unable to respond to the smells left behind for them to answer. Frida whines after a bit and I let her walk again. She has messages to answer.

We had to wait for the surgery since the orthopedic vet wasn't available for two weeks. Frida couldn't see Creek and Mazzy anymore. My vet called and said the orthopedic mobile vet had a cancellation and can do the surgery in Fort Collins in three days. I skipped Pilates class and the monthly office sales meeting and sat at home on the patio with my phone and coffee after I dropped her off at 7:30 a.m. to prep for surgery at 10:00 a.m. The surgeon called me at 10:15, cheery and upbeat, and addressed me as Frida's mom.

"Yes, yes, I am," I practically shouted into the phone. How could the surgery only take fifteen minutes? She must be dead, or they chopped off her leg. I wished I still smoked.

He explained that he started early and did both procedures. Both went well. Frida would be very sore for a while since he had to make a seriously deep groove on the thigh bone to keep the patella in place and staple the cruciate ligament in two different places. But she was awake and hungry.

"She's a very pretty dog and so smart," he said to me. I wondered if that's what he tells every dog mom.

Later, in our post-surgical world, I crafted a new command for Frida: "Put your foot down!" If it were up to Frida, she'd spend the rest of her life as a tripod—a three-legged dog, unfazed by the inconvenience but soon to be challenged by the inevitability that her other rear leg would need similar surgery. Within a week and a thousand treats, Frida put her tender leg down when commanded.

It's part of her rehab to begin the process of using the leg as normally as possible. She also can't run the yard free and fast, prepared to defend the trees and flowers and flagstone patio she has commandeered. She has to be on the end of a leash out in the yard, subject to my ability to stay outside for however long she wants to sniff out the squirrels who have run rampant on her territory, or the bunnies that have scampered free of fear, or the snakes that have slithered from under the old concrete patio and danced in the moonlight. I could tell she was pissed.

Eventually, I tied a twenty-foot leash to a fifteen-pound barbell stopping her from running across the lawn when an errant squirrel chatters at her from the fence. But I was still nearby ready to grab the black cloth leash and stop her from overtaxing the leg. I occasionally yelled, "Put your foot down!" She'd lower it slowly, refusing to look at me.

I love her so much.

* * *

I mixed up my physical therapy appointments with Frida's rehab appointments. Next time, I swear I'll get it right. Frida loves the rehab vet despite what she makes her do and her inquisitive fingers poking and prodding her knee. Then it's time for a cold laser therapy treatment followed by an underwater treadmill walk.

Massage, private Egoscue training, chiropractic and soon PT again are what I do. Watching Frida elongate her stride easily and less painfully on the treadmill forced me to consider pool walking.

I probably make too much of it but when I was sixteen years old, I was in a bad car accident and broke my kneecap and elbow. Three weeks later, I was out of the hospital with a cast on my right arm, one crutch and no cast on my right leg which looked like I contracted polio while I was in the hospital. It was thin and had lost any definition I gained from playing basketball, biking and wandering the town without a car. No one mentioned the possibility of rehab or strengthening my leg. Recently, I wrote an essay about gender bias in the medical community during the time a half-century ago when I had those injuries. Back then, I should've had rehab; they should've cared my leg couldn't hold its own.

Two days later, I broke the kneecap again; it was just a slight give, a momentary lapse in understanding what the knee was supposed to do. I heard it crack. The surgeon scolded me for partying while I stared back not comprehending that I fractured the damn thing again with a slight jarring of the leg. I didn't even fall. I blamed him for his lousy surgical skills and demanded Mom sue him to no avail. The truth was no one cared to rehab my knee. I was a girl and 1960's girl's high school basketball didn't count toward the definition of being an athlete. I still want to sue him and his colleagues, but they're all dead now.

It's why I worry about Frida. Am I doing enough? Should I spend more time with her exercises at home? Will she get arthritis in ten years and be back at rehab, gliding in the underwater treadmill, trying to ease the pain in her joints and maintain some mobility?

At three years old, Frida is about twenty-eight in human years. She easily has at least twelve more years. She deserves a human who can still walk her along the Poudre River, hike a few mountain paths, and bike to Old Town for ice cream. I accept my fate—our fate—that physical therapy and daily exercise need to be penciled in the calendar for the next many-odd years. The sixty dollars a month I pay for her pet insurance is worth many times her eighteen pounds in gold.

Maybe by the time we're old, CBD will be covered by Medicare and Frida's health insurance.

Maybe by then, I'll have that home by the ocean, and we can spend the long days of a Cape Cod summer immersed in the sea, then later in the evening, in the warm waters of our own therapy pool. Maybe by then, we'll find a way for our dogs to live longer, granting us enough time so dog and human can take their last walks along a river or deserted beach—together.

Epilogue

More dogs keep appearing in my life. My son Dan has Hank and now Lily. Sarah adopted Creek while Mazzy was still around to teach him manners. Just a month ago she adopted Teddy, a six-month old gorgeous but malnourished German Shepherd/Malamute mix who is obsessed with Frida. I allowed my downstairs tenant—for the first time—to have a dog so now Piper bursts through the doggie door with the enthusiasm only a young Australian Shepherd can muster.

I don't really *want* more dogs. When I started this book, I hoped to warn people about having too many dogs. I wanted to tell people that dogs can't replace a long-term intimate relationship with a human. I wanted to tell them—as much as I or we love dogs—too many of them keep us from engaging in the wide world of our fellow human beings.

They cost us money, destroy our stuff, and cause us to worry if we've been gone too long as we imagine puddles of urine or a bloodied battle back at the homestead.

Whenever someone asks me what it was like to have three dogs, I'd answer, "Hell." If they asked about getting a third or fourth dog, I'd tell them, "No, you'll regret it." I'd repeat the story of Sunny, whose bad habits and stubbornness motivated me to try to give him away.

I'd show the receipts for my new carpet which I replaced twice. Then the receipt for the cork flooring. Finally, the receipt for the vinyl planking which was installed wrong but works for the most part.

Then I'd bring out the receipt for my six-thousand-dollar yard and its frequent cost of upkeep. I have a running tally of all my dogs' medical bills. During the last ten years it was over twenty-thousand dollars. Though I would mention I was smart enough to invest in pet insurance for everyone and my real costs were a lot less.

I intended to warn the public of the dangers inherent in having too many dogs. The one time I joined Match.com, I mentioned dogs but not how many. Two seems to be acceptable but three borders on obsession. It's not difficult to imagine a potential partner looking at my profile with my arms around three terriers and taking a nanosecond to decide I was a nut case.

I can't tabulate the decreasing efforts I made to connect socially, but it worried me. And here may be the crux of the story. A chicken and egg comparison—what comes first? My natural inclination to avoid people or my obsession with odd and needy dogs?

Would I have been a different person without so many dogs in my life?

I'll never know, but I do know I'm happy because of them. Their existence forced me to be a better person, like Jack Nicholson's character said to Helen Hunt's character in *As Good as It Gets.*

"You make me want to be a better man."

When I first heard that quote, I thought of my dogs. I

wanted to be a better human for them. I also wanted to rescue all the dogs that needed a place to call home. And if I can't rescue them all—I wanted others to rescue them.

Sometimes when I'm walking Frida at Riverbend Ponds, I encounter people with a beautiful dog, and I ask where they got their canine buddy. I can see their hesitation if the dog was from a breeder. They can tell Frida is a mashup of many breeds and maybe they look at me and assume I'm going to yell at them for not getting a rescue, but I'm not. There *are* good breeders out there!

But they don't sell their dogs to pet stores. A friend once invited me to an event at a fellow real estate agent's house and one of the attendee's wife was extolling the virtues of their recently acquired 'designer breed' puppy from a local pet store. My friend put her hand on my arm cautioning me not to say anything. I ignored her and asked if the puppy had been feeling sick lately. I told her it wasn't unusual for these pups to be sick especially since most of them were from a puppy mill where the breeder dogs were neglected and abused. It didn't go over well.

Despite all the protests I've attended at pet stores, I'm not against professional breeders. They love their dogs and are careful about who buys their dogs. But too many people see a bargain Golden Retriever online and don't know they are buying from a backyard breeder or a well-disguised puppy mill. So, when I hear "Oh, he was a very nice breeder, though he wanted us to meet in a parking lot which was odd," I have to walk away.

I've questioned my life with dogs and wondered if they were a crutch for me, using them as an excuse to leave a party or not go on trips or to stay home on holidays. Maybe people would see themselves in my stories and re-think some of their dog decisions.

But the truth is, I wouldn't have changed a thing. If people want to add to their at-home zoo, I'm all for it. If they spend their retirement money on much-needed medical attention for their dog or cat or Vietnamese Pot-Bellied Pig, no worries. They'll just have to work a couple of extra years. If someone finds comfort in a sleeping dog taking up most of their bed space, they've found the answer to insomnia.

I thought something was wrong with me that I had so many dogs, that I kept adopting the crazy ones, or the needy ones, or the ones that might get left behind if I didn't choose them. A few people told me I had a problem when I adopted Sunny or kept Devil Dog Jake or spent my car money to pay for vet bills. There were times I believed them.

But I didn't have a problem. I had an answer. Admittedly, it's not a perfect answer. Dogs die on me all the time and I grieve more often than a human should. But I smile more, and I'm not as tightly wound as I could be. Or as lonely as I thought I would be. When Frida climbs on my lap and settles in, I'm grateful.

Being alone is my default position, not having the courage or ambition or strength to weather an intimate human relationship anymore. I waver between wanting a companion to share my life and not wanting to accommodate another person's needs or frailties. According to any number of spiritual teachings, living with another human would be good practice for me to do if I ever hoped to achieve a modicum of enlightenment.

But some of us are destined to navigate the human experience without a human by our side. I'm okay with that. I will never be okay without a dog to walk the trails with or to share my bed, careful to adjust my sleeping position so I don't disturb the Princes and Princesses (or Queens).

I intend to live a long, healthy life and find myself more great dogs. We'll walk together on the Poudre River Trail every day and watch the river's level rise in the spring and slow to a trickle in early fall.

If you see me with an old dog or two on the trail, say hi and introduce yourself to me and the splendid dogs by my side. But don't worry about our slow gait or our frequent stops to rest on the benches the city has provided.

We'll be okay. We'll find our way home. It's easy when the path is covered in dog hair.

What Little I Know About Dogs...

My sister Nancy and her husband Rick texted me a photo of Adorable Annie, the Staffordshire Terrier they hope to adopt. After filling out an application and providing references, there were two home visits with Annie and a visit to the foster home where Annie lived. Two weeks later, they had a new dog.

They also got a packet of information listing Annie's shots, a wellness check, date of spay or neuter if the rescue paid for it, and her implanted identification chip. There were notes from her foster mom about her behavior and information about her past. In the back of the folder were pamphlets for pet insurance, heartworm pills, flea medications, and a coupon for dog food. This is how it works when you get a rescue dog from a legitimate rescue group.

Four years ago, I had gone to see a couple of dogs at a foster home and had no intention of taking the leap yet. It was too early. It had only been five months since Sunny, the last of the terriers, had died.

But one of the dogs caught my eye. Frida was gorgeous. And friendly. We hung out in the yard, and I threw her a toy. She was another terrier and perfect. Pretty soon, I was rocking Frida like a baby when the foster mom handed me one of her extra leashes.

"Do you want me to walk her?" I intentionally did not bring a leash. It wasn't time to get a dog.

The woman laughed and told me to keep the leash while she handed over Frida's recent medical records and coupons for dog food. I laughed, too, and handed over my credit card.

Years ago, when Dan and I picked up Dylan, our Husky/Yellow Lab mix, we drove to the foster home in the next town over. I knocked on the door and a woman came out with a dog as big as pony while clouds of cigarette smoke enveloped them like the dirt that hovered over Pig-Pen in the Peanuts cartoon. She had told me over the phone he was "maybe fifty pounds" and guessing around three to four years old. He was huge, a conservative eighty pounds. And he was NOT three or four. Double that.

The woman asked for my check and if I had a leash as she unclipped hers. We had just gone over there to meet the dog, not come home with it. I pulled out my checkbook and put Dylan in the car. I feared he would die of lung cancer if I didn't grab him.

Not all rescues are perfect. And neither is the dog-loving public, but there are some things we can do to ensure success for everyone—but mostly for the dog.

1. Be honest about your lifestyle. If you aren't already walking/hiking/biking or SOME movement every day, don't assume your dog is going to be the ONE THING that gets you to exercise.

2. You really need to be screened. I know you're a decent human, but psychopaths can mimic good qualities, too. Not that *you* do. But you may not be ready for a dog. You might be moving or lost a loved one or are temporarily adrift. Not that a

dog couldn't help you with that, but understand a dog is at least a ten-year commitment. If you're lucky.

3. Is the rescue a nonprofit in good standing? Do they have a Board? Do you know anyone on the Board? Are they associated with a trainer and a vet? Find people who have rescued a dog from them and ask about their experience.

4. I read a suggestion that you should take a trainer with you when you visit a potential new furry friend, especially an adult dog. That's genius. It will cost you some money up front but might save some heartache in the future. Some people think they're The Dog Whisperer and claim they 'know' a dog. Just no. You're not.

5. Many rescues don't have a brick-and-mortar building where they house their dogs. That's okay. I like the idea that dogs are in a foster home, dealing with the noise and chaos of a normal household with kids and other dogs. But ask politely if you can come in and visit. If they won't let you, ask why. Dylan's foster mom said it was too chaotic in her house. I believed her after hearing the yapping of at least ten Chihuahuas, but I knew whatever I saw would be upsetting and it wouldn't matter to me, anyway. Dylan was mine.

6. I walk a lot with my dog. As does half of Fort Collins. As our dogs assess each other, the humans partake of pleasant conversation until I mention pet insurance. A few people tell me how much it's helped but the majority of folks don't think it's worth it.

IT'S WORTH IT!

I didn't get pet insurance until the last four dogs. I paid a discount fee for multiple dogs at one hundred and ten dollars a month for years. Then they started falling apart. First it was dental extractions, then abdominal surgeries, glaucoma, eye removal, then painful degenerative disc disease for Zach, severe pancreatitis for Sadie, and bowel cancer for Sunny. In the last months of their lives, there were ultrasounds, soft tissue laser therapy, PT, etc. I went a little overboard. Then there were the costs of euthanasia and cremation.

I had vet appointments every week for the last couple of years with them. Without pet insurance, the cost would have been more than twenty-thousand dollars. With it, my cost was two thousand dollars plus the monthly payments and deductibles which were approximately eight thousand dollars over a number of years. True, I could have had dogs with fewer issues and the cost of the payments and deductibles could have been 'wasted.' But we never know what's going to happen. Having insurance brought me peace, knowing I wouldn't have had to make a difficult choice like dealing with Sunny's painful glaucoma or putting him down.

Today I take Frida to rehab twice a month for her degenerative disc disease, something I may do for the rest of her life. She also did rehab for both knee surgeries. She had a cracked lower canine tooth and had surgery and a bone graft. All expensive procedures done within the first two years of our relationship.

I don't ever want to choose between dealing with my dog's medical issues or letting her suffer. Or worse.

7. If you do go to a breeder, make sure it's a professional breeder. Google how to find one and don't be fooled by breeders whose only claim to professionalism is being AKC-approved. Ask them if they'll take the dog back if there is something wrong. If the breeder hesitates, leave. ALL professional breeders will take your dog back no matter what. No matter how old. They may work with rescues to find them a good home, but they will take their dogs back. Their dogs are family, and you always take care of family. My ex got his dog when a six-year-old Pharoah Hound lost his human to cancer. The breeder reached out to a Pharoah Hound rescue and my ex got himself a new buddy.

8. Don't meet the dog at a parking lot. Don't be fooled by a pretty website. Good breeders will want to meet you and for

you to meet the pup's parents. See the medical history. Does this breed require hip x-rays? Does the breeder give you tons of information about the breed and what makes his pups the best? Does he/she kiss the pup goodbye when you come to pick it up? Good breeders love their dogs and want only the best for them.

* * *

As I write this, I'm watching Ukrainians flee their country, many of them carrying their beloved pets. A lot of them are large dogs either too old or sick or terrified to walk on their own. Their humans drape them across their shoulders—the dog trusting its family will carry it to safety.

I saw a photo of a young woman carrying her older German Shepherd after abandoning the family's car miles from the Polish border. There was another photo of a man crouching over his dog who lay in the street frozen in fear. The man held his dog's head in his hands, talking to him.

I thought about them today when I picked up Frida and carefully placed her across my shoulders, her belly tight against my neck—warm and slightly damp. She was diagnosed recently with the early stages of degenerative disc disease. She's only five. She goes to rehab and walks less than what I want. Today she stops with about a half mile to go. Her pain is catching up to her and I'm happy to carry her the rest of the way. Soon we would get in the car and get a dirty chai tea for me and a puppacino for Frida. How fortunate we are.

One of the first decisions many Americans made at the start of the COVID pandemic was to get a dog. Instinctively we knew unconditional love was going to be necessary in the next few months and possibly years. We knew our hearts might harden and we'd forget how to be tender with ourselves and others. We opened our homes to the one thing that might save us.

Now we watch videos of Ukrainians staying behind and facing the Russian onslaught to care for the dogs and cats in the animal shelters, ensuring they are fed and watered. Two volunteers were killed as they headed back to the shelter with dogs they found scared and running loose in the streets.

I wonder what I would do if I were running from certain death. Frida would come with me but what about other dogs? Would I squeeze them into my Subaru Forester? If we had to walk, could I put the slowest dogs in my large dog jogger, leash the others to its handles, and run as fast as someone who needs a knee replacement can?

God, I hope so.

About the Author

Mary Roberts is a debut author at seventy-one years old with a family lineage of living beyond one hundred. She intends to use those years making up for lost time.

Mary received her BA in Technical Journalism in 1974 and a master's degree in Communication with an emphasis on Creative Nonfiction Writing in 2010.

She did a few things in between. Raised two kids, had a bunch of dogs, taught Kundalini Yoga, personal storytelling, and five-card stud to her grandkids. She has worked as a real estate agent for 24 years. She also competes in story slams and organizes storytelling events to encourage the practice of listening to each other.

Mary started writing 14 Dogs and Me after the death of the Whack Pack, three terrier mixes who died within months of each other. Being without a dog inspired her to see what life would be like without one or two. Turns out, it was terrible. She welcomed Frida into her home five months later.

She writes about dogs, aging, stuttering, and the power of storytelling.

Acknowledgments

I need to apologize to anyone who came over to my house when I had three or more dogs. It was loud and hairy and my dogs were tenacious beggars. Thank you for your patience.

My kids, Sarah April and Dan April, probably think I needed to pay more attention to them than my dogs. In my defense, they both challenged themselves and live interesting and successful lives. AND! They both have multiple dogs! My plan worked!

A huge thank you to Kerrie Flanagan for her editing skills and shepherding me through the world of self-publishing. And to Jennifer Schafer for her artistic vision of my cover, chapter headings, and the fabulous bookmarks!

Gary Kimsey was my editor at The Rocky Mountain Collegian 50 years ago and he was the first person to read the first draft of my book. I must apologize for subjecting him to that and thank him for his kind and insightful edits.

I initially wrote this book to understand why I had so many dogs and why so many of them presented one challenge after the other. After rereading it a few million times, I understand now these dogs were there to make sure my heart never gave up. With much appreciation and love, pups, from your all-too-human Mom.